Goodwill on Two Wheels

Goodwill On Two Wheels

Jamal Hasan

Published as eBook
and
Paperback
By Amazon in 2022

ISBN 978-1-9163808-2-0 (eBook)
ISBN 978-1-9163808-3-7 (Paperback)

Editing services: Writers Services

Design by
eBookpBook

Cover: Imon Hasan

In memory of all freedom fighters
Who made the ultimate sacrifice
For our freedom & happiness.

Acknowledgement

When we enjoy reading a book, do we ever think of the various peoples' contributions behind the scene to make it an enjoyable read? Of course, not. Most authors, if not all, acknowledge only a few people, but I am sure it is beyond any author's ability to mention all the people who helped finalise the manuscript.

Well, I am not an exception. I do not wish to bore my readers with irrelevant information. But at the same time, I do not want to feel like an ungrateful creature by not mentioning the names of very few people without whose support I would have deprived my readers to enjoy this book.

The first name I have to mention is my wife, Gulshan. Not because she is my wife but because it is so true that without her cooperation and support, it would have been impossible for me to finish this book.

The second name is my brother-in-law, Howard Doble, who encouraged me to write about my world cycle tour experience. Unfortunately, for half a century, I could never find the time, nor did I have the will to get on this task, although it has always been in my mind to share the fascinating experience of the world cycle tour. Howard pushed me to start writing this book.

Once I decided to write about the cycle tour and informed my teammates, all of them became happy and encouraged me to go ahead. They told me they were also thinking of writing something on the cycle tour, but somehow, it did not materialise. Nevertheless, they all volunteered to help me in any way they could.

Unfortunately, except for Akhtar, we mislaid our dairies and notes on the cycle tour. Therefore, Akhtar's help gave me the confidence to start writing. However, we live in two different countries. Thus, both Akhtar and I found it difficult to communicate by telephone.

Although Khokan and Babul did not have their dairies handy, they helped me by providing me with important information from their memories.

'Goodwill on Two Wheels' is a memoir. However, I based my story mainly on my experience on the World Cycle Tour. Therefore, I could not write this book without my teammates' help and cooperation. I would particularly like to acknowledge my close friend Akhtar's contributions, for which I am incredibly grateful.

Finally, my deepest thanks go to my two brothers, NM Harun and Abu Musa Hasan, both veteran journalists. Their contributions have been most helpful. My older brother, N M Harun, did a diligent review of the manuscript many times to ensure that my narrative of the political history of Bangladesh was accurate.

I underestimated the amount of admin work I needed to finish the book. Firstly, with my limited knowledge of graphic design, and secondly, because of my poor health conditions, I often felt like giving up the idea of completing the book. However, my elder son, Ishan Hasan, encouraged me to continue. With his advanced computer skills, Ishan has helped me enormously to the end. I am also grateful to my younger son, Imon Hasan, a professional motion graphic designer, for designing the cover pages.

I would also like to thank the following people:

Mr Ashequn Nabi Chowdhury, Press Minister, Bangladesh High Commission, London for permitting me to reproduce articles published in the 'Bangladesh Today' on 15 September 1972 and 1 November 1972.

Mr Omesh Torne of The Free Press Journal, Mumbai, India, for permitting me to reproduce an article published in Free Press Journal 0n 7 June 1972.

Ms Vidya, of ebookpbook. Besides designing 'Goodwill on two Wheels' to the highest standard, she has always been extremely helpful in answering my various questions. I am most grateful to Vidya for advising me on many matters and, sometimes, even carrying out some research work.

My special thanks

While I was a student at Goldsmith College, I had the opportunity to get a work experience placement at the Joint Council for the Welfare of Immigrants (JCWI). In no time, the General Secretary of the JCWI, Ian Martin, became one of my close friends and my mentor in the UK. Ian has always guided me in building my career. On one occasion, Ian advised me not to accept an offer of a very tempting job and asked me to stick to my job at the law centre. Because I listened to his advice, I stuck with the law centre movement and had the most satisfying working life. As a result, when I retired from my job, I was the longest-serving law centre worker in the country.

Ian has had a colourful career. After leaving JCWI, he joined Britain's oldest political think tank organization, the Fabian Society, as the General Secretary. Then, in 1985, he joined Amnesty International, becoming in 1986 its Secretary General. Finally, he got engaged in an enviable career and has been working as a representative of the United Nations.

As a United Nations representative, Ian has always been on the move and travelling all over the world, but we have always remained in touch. We always try to meet and catch up whenever he comes to the UK.

Ian would come up with the right direction whenever I

needed his advice. Before Sir Alec Jeffreys invented DNA testing to scientifically establish the parental relationship, like all immigration law practitioners, I became frustrated for not succeeding with my immigration appeal cases. I discussed with Ian about taking a high-profile individual to Bangladesh for a village visit. Immediately Ian suggested I contact one of his friends, Alf Dubs, MP, (Now Lord Dubs). Because of an unavoidable reason, Alf Dubs could not make it and Frank Dobson, MP, went to Bangladesh with me instead. Out of the 14 cases we investigated, we were satisfied with the claimed relations with all but one family. The British High Commission conceded nine cases and maintained their refusal for five clients. They had to wait until DNA testing was invented!

Ian knew about my world cycle tour. So he was happy when he learnt that I started writing a book about my experience on the world cycle tour. Whenever we communicated by emails or met in London, he would enquire about the book's progress. As it took much longer to finish the book, Ian always pushed me to finish my writing quickly.

Jamal Hasan

Table of Contents

Foreword

On 25 March 1971, I witnessed the tanks rolling out of Dhaka's cantonment into the centre of the city early in the night when the Pakistan Army's killings in East Bengal began. Throughout that night, I watched from a rooftop the firing which was targeting in particular the Hindu quarters of the university and the city, as well as the presumed supporters of independence. Friends whom I had made since I had come to work in undivided Pakistan during what was to be its last year fled to India, and became fighters or campaigners for Bangladesh. I returned to Dhaka in January 1972, only weeks after the liberation of Bangladesh, to experience the first year of its life as an independent country.

Jamal Hasan was not among those I knew in that period; we met only after I had returned to London. We had started to work in different organisations on behalf of families separated by Britain's racially discriminatory immigration procedures, but beyond our professional association we shared with each other our respective experiences of his country and its liberation struggle. Thus I came to know of his inspired bicycle diplomacy.

While waiting in the queue for a place for arms training, Jamal thought of riding for freedom instead. So he decided to go on a world cycle tour to strengthen support from other countries for the liberation war. Happily, when Jamal and his friends were about to start the cycle tour, Bangladesh's independence was achieved. Jamal and his friends then decided instead to set out on a goodwill mission to thank the people of the world for supporting their liberation war. They set out on bicycles to introduce their new country across India and Europe, consolidating the sympathy which they found among leaders and populations.

I always thought this was a story that deserved to be written, and now Jamal has recorded it in this book, illustrating it with some rare contemporary documents and photos. It is a fine reminder of the spirit of young Bengalis and the international solidarity – despite some hostile governments, most notably that of Nixon and Kissinger in the USA – which launched Bangladesh on its path as an independent nation.

Ian Martin

ONE

Dhaka

The night before the big day, I came home quite late. The process of saying goodbye to my friends had taken much longer than expected. My parents and all my brothers and sisters were anxiously waiting for me. I began to feel guilty for coming home so late. 'I am sorry I couldn't come earlier. My friends would not let me leave. We grew up together, and I am leaving them for a long time.'

My younger sister, Husne Ara Helen, would not usually have let me get away with such an excuse. However, that evening was different. Everybody, except our mother, kept quiet while I frantically tried to organise the stuff I would carry.

I looked at the time and was horrified; I feared I did not have enough time to organise everything before going to bed! I tried to keep calm and quell my restlessness. Only our mother was talking; the rest were watching and communicating with me through silent but very engaging looks. Our mother repeatedly asked me to go to bed early and get a good night's sleep. She kept reminding me about the physical strength I would need the next day. My youngest sister, Khaleda Hira, has always been very emotional by nature. Her eyes were wet with tears. She found it extremely difficult to believe I was about to leave them for such a long time.

My mother's continuous talking about the arduous journey I would embark on darkened the atmosphere. 'You must promise that you will always be careful. You must promise that you will always be vigilant.' She kept on repeating the same sentences and occasionally added, 'The journey could be precarious and may be dangerous. You will always have to be alert.' She continuously appealed to me to give her my word. I repeated my assurances that I would always be careful and that she did not have to worry about me. 'I am an adult and capable of looking after myself. Moreover, I will be accompanied by three adult friends. There is nothing you need to worry about. Everything will be fine. I will write to you whenever I have the opportunity.'

While responding to my mother's pleas, I put the important stuff in the small leather box I would carry.

I could not go to bed as early as I had hoped. However, when I finally went to bed very late, I found it extremely difficult to have a sound sleep. I woke up quite early, at 5 am. Immediately I turned off the alarm so that it did not have the chance to make its annoying noise and disturb everybody's sleep. To my surprise, I found everybody in the house was already up!

While I had my breakfast, I asked everybody to say goodbye from the front door and not to follow me to the Prime Minister's Residence, where I would start my world cycle tour with three other friends, Khokan (Anwar Uddin Ahmed), Babul (Mahmud Abdul Quayum) and Akhtar (Syed Akhtar Ali). My parents agreed, but my younger brother and two sisters did not. They were ready to follow me; my brother on his bike and my two sisters on a rickshaw.

The people of Bangladesh were so close to the Prime Minister, Sheikh Mujibur Rahman, that we called him either 'Bangabandhu' (*Friend of Bengal*) or just 'Mujib Bhai' (*Brother Mujib*); rarely did we refer to him as Sheikh Mujibur Rahman.

Akhtar lived a few hundred yards from my house in the same neighbourhood. He was ready and waiting for me. Akhtar's brothers and a small group of our friends had assembled in the field in front of Akhtar's house, all excited and ready to accompany us to the Prime Minister's house on their bikes. We looked like a happy procession of cyclists.

Soon after Akhtar and I reached Bangabandhu's Residence at 32 Dhanmondi Residential Area, Babul and Khokan joined us from their neighbourhoods, each with an entourage. As a result, Bangabandhu's front garden became rather crowded on the early morning of 7 April 1972.

Our Starting point. Our Prime Minister's front Garden

Previously, Bangabandhu had given us a letter asking us to convey his good wishes and greetings to the people of the countries we would visit on our world tour by bicycle.

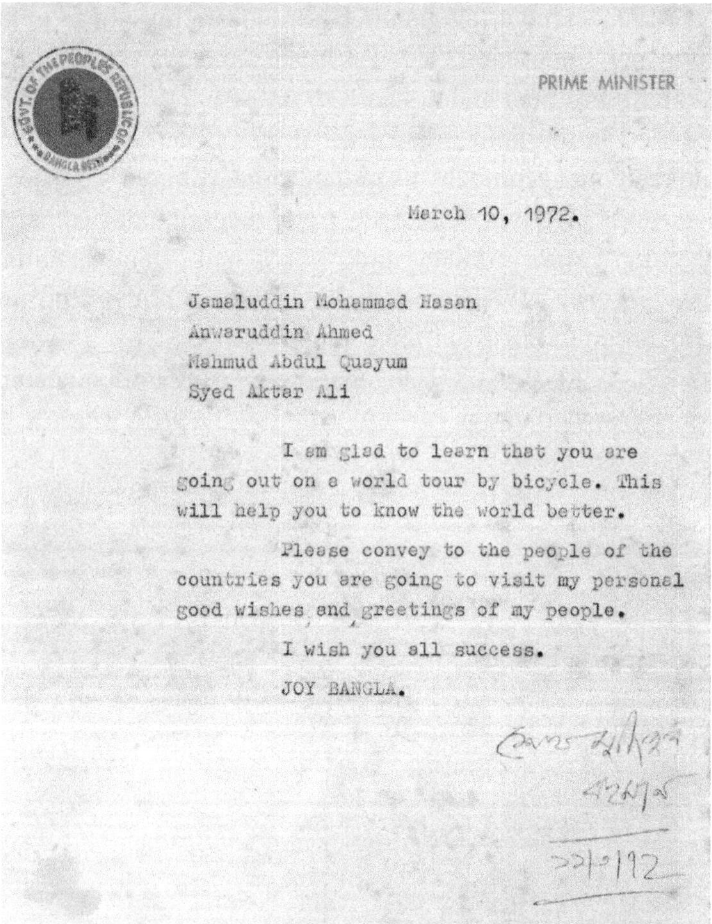

PRIME MINISTER

March 10, 1972.

Jamaluddin Mohammad Hasan
Anwaruddin Ahmed
Mahmud Abdul Quayum
Syed Aktar Ali

I am glad to learn that you are going out on a world tour by bicycle. This will help you to know the world better.

Please convey to the people of the countries you are going to visit my personal good wishes and greetings of my people.

I wish you all success.

JOY BANGLA.

Prime Minister's letter of Good Wishes

Bangabandhu's presence and smiling face removed any anxiety or fear we might have harboured in our minds. His reassuring words were music to our ears. His assurances that no obstacle or difficulty would stand in our way made us feel strong. We no longer had any fear of facing unforeseen problems. Moreover, his occasional witty jokes made us feel light and relaxed and made us forget we were about to start a journey that could be full of hazards. First, he asked us about our route, and then he joked, 'When you leave India, make sure that you do not enter Pakistan by mistake!'

On a serious note, Bangabandhu said, 'Be strong and always feel proud to represent Bangladesh abroad.' Bangabandhu gave us an envelope containing some money. Bangabandhu wished us success and, in a loud voice, said, 'Joy Bangla' (Victory to Bangladesh), exciting the large crowd. We echoed him by screaming our favourite slogan, 'Joy Bangla, Joy Bangla, Joy Bangla...' We waved at the large crowd and started our journey.

'Joy Bangla' has always been a powerful morale-boosting slogan for us, and it had a magical effect on us throughout our independence struggle.

To celebrate Mujib bhai's release from imprisonment by the Pakistan Government in 1969, the All Party Student Action Committee organised a memorable rally at the Ramna race course. People not only from Dhaka city but also from other districts attended this rally. I remember going to the race course quite early to find a space closer to the enormous podium, where approximately 20 people were sitting on chairs waiting for Mujib bhai's arrival.

In this rally, the All Party Student Action Committee gave Mujib bhai the title 'Bangabandhu' (Friend of Bengal). We went wild with excitement and spontaneously screamed at the top of our voices, "Joy Bangla", "Joy Bangla", "Joy Bangla"... Oh, what a scene it was when the sea of people shouted Joy Bangla continuously in all corners of the race course! Since then, "Joy Bangla" has become the pre-eminent slogan of the people of Bangladesh. Later it became the war cry of the Mukti Bahinni (Freedom Fighters) in the Liberation war in 1971. Finally, after independence, Joy Bangla became the national slogan of Bangladesh.

We set off from Bangabandhu's house and made our first stop at the Foreign Minister's Residence in Segun Bagicha. Mr Abdus Samad had given us a letter of recommendation.

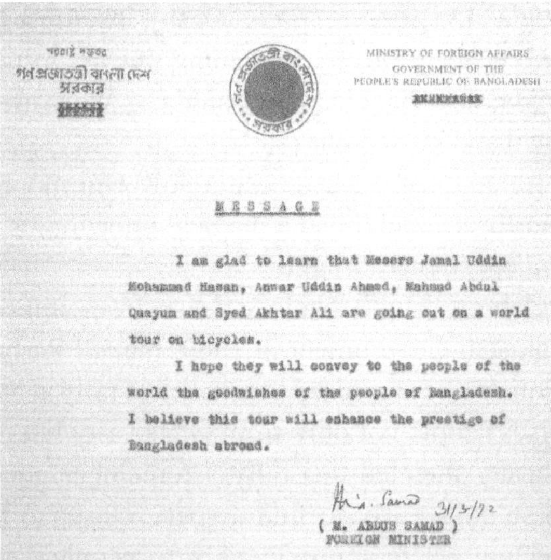

গণপ্রজাতন্ত্রী বাংলা দেশ
সরকার

MINISTRY OF FOREIGN AFFAIRS
GOVERNMENT OF THE
PEOPLE'S REPUBLIC OF BANGLADESH

MESSAGE

I am glad to learn that Messrs Jamal Uddin Mohammad Hasan, Anwar Uddin Ahmed, Mahmud Abdul Quayum and Syed Akhtar Ali are going out on a world tour on bicycles.

I hope they will convey to the people of the world the goodwishes of the people of Bangladesh. I believe this tour will enhance the prestige of Bangladesh abroad.

31/3/72

(M. ABDUS SAMAD)
FOREIGN MINISTER

Foreign Minister's letter of recommendation

Ministry of Foreign Minister, had already written to all Bangladesh Missions abroad requesting to extend consular facilities to us.

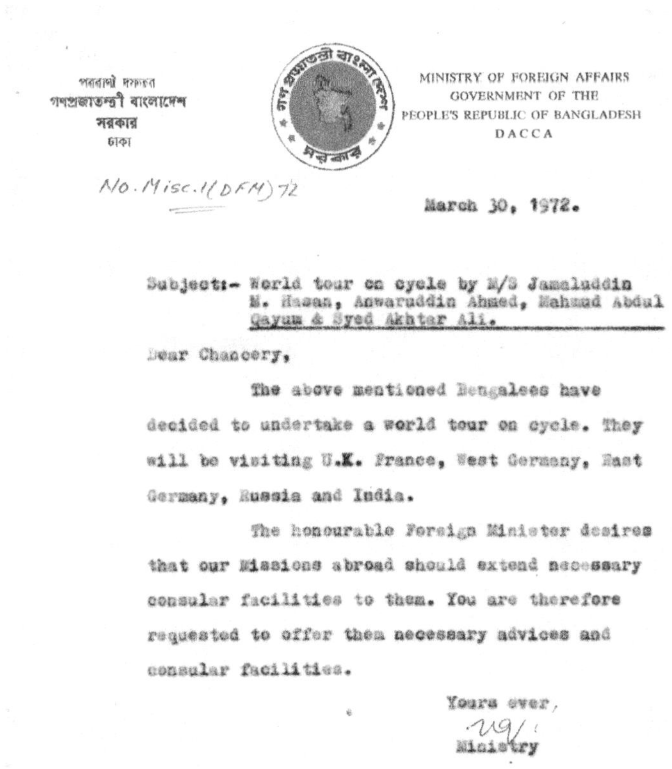

পররাষ্ট্র দফতর
গণপ্রজাতন্ত্রী বাংলাদেশ
সরকার
ঢাকা

MINISTRY OF FOREIGN AFFAIRS
GOVERNMENT OF THE
PEOPLE'S REPUBLIC OF BANGLADESH
DACCA

No. Misc.1(DFM)72

March 30, 1972.

Subject:- World tour on cycle by M/S Jamaluddin M. Hasan, Anwaruddin Ahmed, Mahmud Abdul Qayum & Syed Akhtar Ali.

Dear Chancery,

The above mentioned Bengalees have decided to undertake a world tour on cycle. They will be visiting U.K. France, West Germany, East Germany, Russia and India.

The honourable Foreign Minister desires that our Missions abroad should extend necessary consular facilities to them. You are therefore requested to offer them necessary advices and consular facilities.

Yours ever,

Ministry

Letter from the ministry of Foreign affairs, to Bangladesh Missions asking to extend consular facilities to us.

Like Bangabandhu, the Foreign Minister also gave us lots of helpful advice. Then he inspired us by saying, 'Do not forget, you are the roving ambassadors of Bangladesh.' He reminded us that it was our duty to represent Bangladesh abroad in the best possible way. Finally, he also gave us an envelope containing some money and said, 'Best wishes for a successful world tour.'

After saying our goodbyes, we started our journey, following the Aricha Road.

After a while, we stopped and asked those of our friends who were still following us to return home. We didn't want to turn them away, but we needed to concentrate on our journey. We shouted, 'Joy Bangla,' and now it felt like we had really started our tour.

We decided to stop over at Akhtar's village, Kashiani, in the Faridpur district. Faridpur is about seventy-five miles from Dhaka. It was not a detour; Faridpur was on the route to Kolkata. Akhtar's wife, Dilara Bhabi, had travelled to Kashiani with their daughter, Leeta, to receive us there.

The weather turned bad on us, and Dilara Bhabi's hospitality was irresistible, so we ended up staying in Kashiani for an extra day. We left Faridpur on 9 April 1971 and headed towards Kolkata.

Soon we were on the picturesque Jessore Road. Cycling here was a pleasant experience, with green trees lined up on both sides, making a scenic arch above us; but most importantly, it was blissfully flat, the ideal road for cycling. Later, when we struggled to ride on the hilly roads in Europe, we missed the Jessore Road.

On the Jessore Road

We had been hoping for a dry, hot day so we could enjoy this beautiful road to the full. Instead, it was a dull day with mild drizzle. The road became slippery, slowing us down. Suddenly, Khokan's bike skidded, and he fell into a roadside ditch. We panicked when we found a sharp date tree thorn embedded in his leg. We struggled to remove the thorn and immediately decided to take Khokan to the nearest hospital. This incident, right at the start of our odyssey, deflated us a little; but it was only temporary.

While we took an enforced break, we thoroughly checked our bikes and made sure they were in top condition.

Giving a thorough check of our bikes.

Long after our tour ended, I discovered that the story of how Jessore road came to be was more interesting than the road itself. I learnt that it was created by an affluent goldsmith from the Jessore District, Mr Kali Prasad Poddar, and a consequence of his unparalleled love for his mother.

One day in 1826, Mr Poddar's mother asked him to improve the road from Jessore to Kolkata. She frequently visited Kolkata to bathe in the sacred water of the holy Ganges. However, she always had a very uncomfortable journey because of the rough road. So Mr Poddar's mother also asked him to plant trees on both sides of the road so that the trees would shade her on hot summer days.

Mr Poddar got on with the task of improving the road

without delay. It was a Herculean task; the road is one hundred and twenty kilometres long. He had thousands of trees planted on both sides of the road, as his mother had requested. Eventually, after five years of hard work, the project was completed. Mr Poddar gave it its name, and the rest is history. It makes for a beautiful journey; in the hot summer, travellers can enjoy their journey under the sweet shade of the trees, just as Mr Poddar intended.

HM Government awarded Mr Poddar the title of 'Chowdhury' for building the massive and impressive road. Chowdhury is not just an Indian surname but a title of honour derived from ancient Sanskrit.

Unfortunately, this beautiful, shady road, and the sweet story of its creation, was recently threatened with destruction. The authorities, driven by commercial interests and without regard for the love story or the environment, decided to chop down the century-old trees on Jessore Road. However, environmentalists all over the country mounted a strong campaign and forced the authorities to change their minds.

So Jessore road is not just a symbol of Kali Prasad Poddar's love for his mother. It also reminds everybody of the importance of opposition and involvement in campaigning for good causes.

Along our route from Dhaka to Kolkata, we were horrified to see mass graves and human remains constantly reminding us of this dark chapter in our history. These scenes reminded us of two events: one in 1947 and the other only a year earlier, in 1971.

We became emotional seeing the mass graves

We remembered, with the most profound sadness, the biggest communal riots the world had ever seen, in 1947, when India was partitioned based on religion. Then, less than twenty-five years later, we became victims of the horrific genocide committed by the brutal Pakistani army. Once again, millions of innocent Bangladeshis lost their lives. This time, however, we were not saddened but enraged and were determined to drive away the occupying Pakistan army from our motherland and to set ourselves free from exploitation and injustice. We did not do this alone. With few exceptions, the whole world supported our determination to liberate ourselves from Pakistan. Our cycle tour was meant to thank the world for its support in our liberation struggle.

The Background

After the partition of India in 1947, Pakistan was created for the Muslim population. We, in the Bengal, were called East Pakistan, and over 1000 miles away in the western region of India were called West Pakistan. Pakistan's ruling clique treated East Pakistan as their colony. They exploited us beyond human limits. They even tried to impose a foreign language on us. It was horribly frustrating for a people and a culture that forms the majority in a country to be violently dominated and exploited by the minority. We never had a honeymoon period, and it was only a matter of time before we would be separated and divorced.

Twenty-three years after independence from Britain, the first general elections were held in Pakistan in December 1970. Bangabandhu, the leader of the Awami League party, won a decisive majority. However, Pakistan would not accept the election results, and they immediately started to hatch plots to undermine the people's choices. Pakistan's ruling clique was not prepared to give up the power they had enjoyed since 1947. They made it clear that they would continue to rule us by force.

7 April 1972 was a big day for the four of us when we started our world cycle tour from the unofficial Residence of the father of the nation, Bangabandhu Sheikh Mujibur Rahman. However, we could never forget one of the most critical days in Bangladesh's political calendar, precisely

a year and a month earlier. It was on 7 March 1971 when Bangabandhu, in a famous speech, told us that our struggle was no longer to gain our legitimate rights from Pakistan; it was a struggle for the independence of Bangladesh. Bangabandhu advised us to transform our homes into fortresses. We became inspired and sincerely believed that independence was within our reach. After that speech, the political temperature quickly rose. Extraordinary events followed one after another. We mounted a successful non-cooperation movement. Everything was closed down, and there was no effective Pakistani Government administration in the whole country, particularly in East Pakistan. We only followed the directives from Bangabandhu. We barricaded the roads so the army could not move around in the city.

In response, the Pakistan military junta drafted enormous army personnel from West Pakistan into Bangladesh. As a result, the situation became increasingly tense.

On 23 March 1971, I went to my ancestral home, a village called Raitola, in Brahmonbaria, for a few days. Two days after I left Dhaka, in the middle of the night of 25 March, the Pakistan army launched a crackdown and killed many innocent Bangladeshis in their sleep. Army tanks patrolled the streets. The killing rampage continued throughout the night, and the army imposed an indefinite curfew. No one knew if their friends or relatives had survived the horrible onslaught. Later we discovered that, although the army was killing innocent Bangladeshis indiscriminately, they also had a few specific targets. They targeted the East Pakistan Rifles (EPR), now Border Guard of Bangladesh

(BGB), the Rajarbag Police Line and the university dormitories at Dhaka, notably Jagannath Hall, the Residence for the Hindus and other minority students of Dhaka University.

As soon as the army lifted the curfew for a few hours, most people who were able to escape got out of Dhaka city as quickly as they could. However, nobody had the time to plan their escape; most people who left Dhaka carried nothing and were separated from their loved ones. No one had a specific destination; they just wanted to escape the killing fields. Although everybody was heading in different directions, they had one ultimate common goal: to prepare themselves for the mother of all liberation wars against the mighty Pakistani army.

The news of the army crackdown spread all over Bangladesh with lightning speed. I was horrified to hear the word of the cowardly and heinous acts perpetrated by the Pakistan army. There was no way I could get any information about my parents and all my close relatives. All of us were glued to the radio, night and day, listening to Akashbani Kolkata, BBC and Voice of America, the only sources of information.

It did not take us long to realise that young people all over the country were becoming freedom fighters, eager to resist the Pakistan army's attack. I met several young students who had managed to escape from their usual residences in Dhaka and other cities and had returned to the village to escape from the atrocities of the Pakistan army. Everybody was gearing up to get involved in the resistance movement.

Very quickly, the whole country started experiencing the

atrocities of the Pakistan army. We realised that it was no longer just inside Dhaka and the major cities of the land; even the deep interior of the country became targets of the army. So naturally, we felt fear and horror when we started seeing dead bodies floating past us in the floodwater. However, the more we realised the extent of the atrocities of the Pakistan army, the more determined we were to combat the army's occupation of our motherland.

As soon as I learnt that young people were being encouraged to go to India to get arms training, I pressed the young and able people in our village to go to Agartala, only a few miles away from us. Before I went to India, I wanted to mobilise the maximum number of potential fighters.

Because of my involvement in student politics, I had the expertise to write leaflets/posters and graffiti on walls. I teamed up with the young boys who had come to the village to protect their lives. We bought the necessary materials, including carbon paper, to produce leaflets and started distributing these leaflets in the markets where people would assemble. After leafleting in the neighbouring markets, we visited the big markets close to our village. We were impressed to see the enthusiasm in most people. They had already undergone mental preparation and were determined to join the armed struggle.

One day I was campaigning in a big town called Nabinagar when I was overjoyed to see my parents, two sisters and one brother boarding a boat to our village. My parents told me that my eldest sister and her family had escaped from Dhaka, but unfortunately, they did not know their whereabouts.

Until that day, I had not known that my close relatives had survived the army onslaught. It took nearly three weeks for my parents to make it approximately seventy-five miles to reach Nabinagar. They had to stop at different places and often could not continue the journey because of the army activities.

Soon we heard that the army was constantly patrolling the Brahmanbaria – Comilla road (now the Sylhet Comilla Road), and crossing this road was becoming increasingly dangerous. The Indian border was only three/four miles from the Sylhet- Comilla Road, but as we were situated on the west side, we could not travel east to Agartala without crossing this road. I felt terribly frustrated; I had helped two big groups of young men cross the border when it was relatively easy to walk into India. I thought it was essential to mobilise more people before I left, but now I started to course myself, fearing that I might be stuck in the village. Besides me, a few other friends had also become desperate to go to Agartala and participate actively in the armed struggle. It quickly became boring to spend every day engaged only in armchair politics.

My younger brother had already managed to go to Agartala with a group of volunteers. Eventually, with a few other friends, I became so desperate to go to Agartala that we decided to take the risk of making the journey and actively participate in the armed struggle.

TWO

Agartala

While I was stuck in the village without seeing any prospect of escaping the situation, I felt that guerrilla war was not enough, on its own, to defeat the Pakistan army. It was essential to get international support for our cause. I remembered the conflict in Vietnam, which had been going on since my teens. I realised it might take a long time to oust the Pakistan army from our motherland. At that time, no country had recognised our declaration of independence. However, India was sympathetic to our cause and drew the world's attention to the genocide in Bangladesh. India also opened its borders to Bangladeshi refugees.

There were four of us, still in the village, who decided to run the risk of going to Agartala; we knew it would be highly dangerous. So one night, after midnight, we got in a boat and headed towards the Sylhet-Comilla road. As soon as we were close to the main road, we stopped, camouflaged ourselves with water plants and, instead of using the oars, we made the boat move forward slowly by using our hands. When we noticed an army vehicle on the road with the head-lights on full beam, we stopped all movement and remained wholly motionless until the soldiers disappeared.

Because of the high water level, the Tinlakhpir Bridge

seemed very low. We lay flat in the boat to ensure we did not hit the bridge in the dark. We took a deep breath as we passed underneath the bridge. After that scary moment, we felt like we were in a safe zone; the other side of the road was still in East Pakistan (now Bangladesh), and the Indian border was still a few miles away. However, psychologically we were relieved to have crossed the bridge, and we gradually speeded up until we found a place to land. We felt indestructible as if nothing could happen to us. There were mixed feelings when we finally put our feet on Indian soil. We were out of the Pakistan army's range, and that was a great relief. However, we realised that we were now refugees in a foreign country. Knowing that India was a friendly country, vocal in supporting our fight for independence, made us feel better.

My three companions decided to look for their relatives and close friends who had made the journey earlier. I said goodbye to them and concentrated on searching for a refugee camp. Finally, someone led me to a place that did not look like a refugee camp. Instead, it appeared to be a neat, attractive building with gardens.

I went in nervously, fearing that the stranger had misinformed me about this place, but I saw some familiar faces as soon as I went in. They were acquaintances from Dhaka University. None of them was from my department, but we frequently bumped into each other in the common room or the canteen. Seeing them, I was hugely reassured, knowing that I was not with a group of strangers. However, the biggest surprise was waiting in the wings for me. Suddenly I saw one of my nieces, Annie or Bani, coming out of a room.

Before I could open my mouth, my niece screamed with joy and shouted to her mum, 'Ammo, come out and see who is here!' My sister and the rest of her family members appeared at once. We were taken aback and, for a moment, speechless.

Looking back at how events unfolded for me from then on, I now realise how fortunate I was. I knew that my maternal grandfather, Mr Gulam Rabbani, had lived in Agartala and had been a teacher at the Raj Bari School. However, I did not know that the Chief Minister of Agartala, Mr Sachindra Lal Singh, and the elected Lok Sabha (Indian Parliament) member from Agartala, Mr Biren Dutta, had been my grandfather's students. My maternal uncle, who was already in Agartala, was staying with Biren Dutta's older brother, Mr Dhiren Dutta. My sister would visit Dhiren and Biren Dutta's families now and then. Dhiren Dutta's son, Subir Dutta, was the same age as me and used to come to see my older sister to enquire if she needed anything. In fact, Dihiren Dutta helped my sister to get a place in the camp, which was a hostel of the Agartala Arts College. No wonder the place was so neat and clean.

I learned from the other residents in the camp that it was not easy to get a place in a training camp; all of them were full. This information was a catalyst for my plan to go abroad.

Subir would always go to any lengths to help us. So, when I told him that I was planning to go on a world tour by bicycle to strengthen international support for the cause of Bangladesh, he became very excited and wanted to help me in any way he could.

It had been quite a long time since my grandfather left Agartala, but almost everybody remembered him with respect. Because I was the grandson of Mr Gulam Rabbani,

I had a great advantage. I met some important people in Agartala. Amongst them were Mr Sudhir Ranjan Majumdar, President of the Agartala Congress Committee (the ruling political party of India at that time). Sudhir Ranjan Majumdar gave us a letter of introduction:

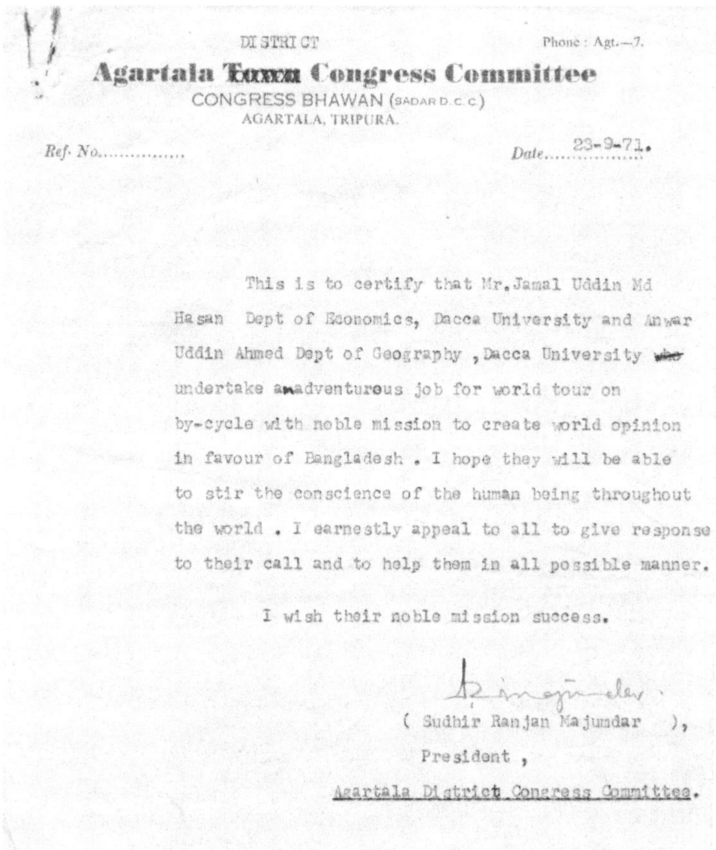

DISTRICT

Phone : Agt.—7.

Agartala ~~Town~~ Congress Committee

CONGRESS BHAWAN (SADAR D.C.C.)

AGARTALA, TRIPURA.

Ref. No................. *Date*.....23-9-71.

This is to certify that Mr. Jamal Uddin Md Hasan Dept of Economics, Dacca University and Anwar Uddin Ahmed Dept of Geography, Dacca University ~~who~~ undertake an adventureous job for world tour on by-cycle with noble mission to create world opinion in favour of Bangladesh. I hope they will be able to stir the conscience of the human being throughout the world. I earnestly appeal to all to give response to their call and to help them in all possible manner.

I wish their noble mission success.

(Sudhir Ranjan Majumdar),

President,

Agartala District Congress Committee.

Mr Majumdar's letter of introduction

Mr Santi Pada Chowdhury also given us an inspiring letter of introduction:

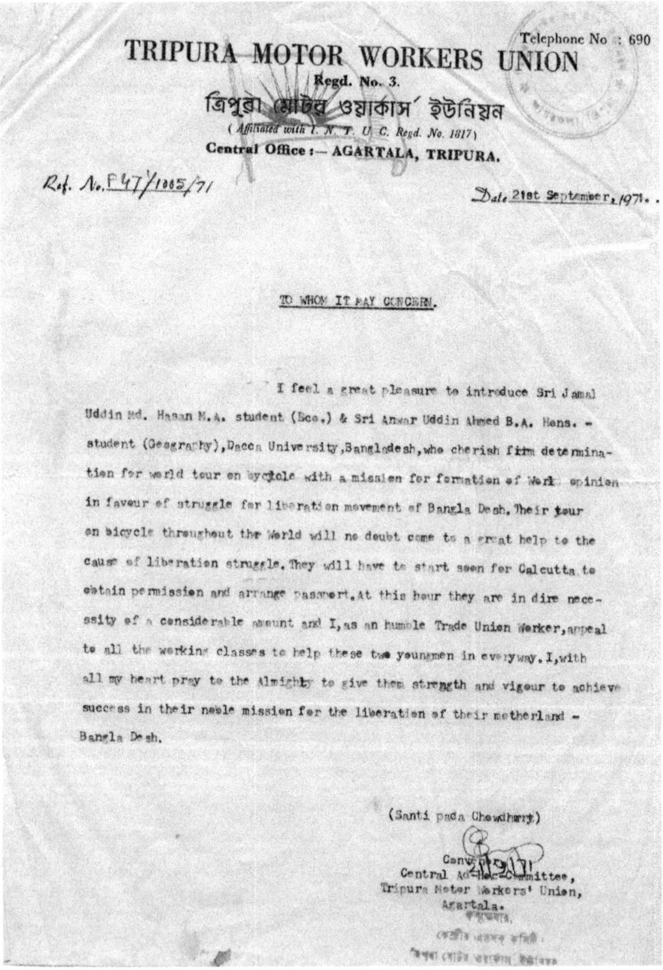

TRIPURA MOTOR WORKERS UNION

Telephone No : 690

Regd. No. 3.

ত্রিপুরা মোটর ওয়ার্কার্স ইউনিয়ন

(*Affiliated with I. N. T. U. C. Regd. No. 1817*)

Central Office :— AGARTALA, TRIPURA.

Ref. No. F47/1365/71

Date 21st September, 1971.

TO WHOM IT MAY CONCERN.

I feel a great pleasure to introduce Sri Jamal Uddin Md. Hasan M.A. student (Eco.) & Sri Anwar Uddin Ahmed B.A. Hons. - student (Geography), Dacca University, Bangladesh, who cherish firm determination for world tour on bycycle with a mission for formation of World opinion in favour of struggle for liberation movement of Bangla Desh. Their tour on bicycle throughout the World will no doubt come to a great help to the cause of liberation struggle. They will have to start soon for Calcutta to obtain permission and arrange passport. At this hour they are in dire necessity of a considerable amount and I, as an humble Trade Union Worker, appeal to all the working classes to help these two youngmen in everyway. I, with all my heart pray to the Almighty to give them strength and vigour to achieve success in their noble mission for the liberation of their motherland - Bangla Desh.

(Santi pada Chowdhury)
21/9/71
Convener,
Central Ad-Hoc-Committee,
Tripura Motor Workers' Union,
Agartala.

Mr Santi Pada's letter of introduction

Tripura Workers Union were extremely helpful and agreed to help me get my world tour project off the ground.

One day my cousin, Khokan, who was staying in another refugee camp, came to see my older sister. He was excited to see me there so unexpectedly. When I told him I was planning to go on a world tour by bicycle to get support for our liberation war, he was surprised to hear my ambitious plan and said he would love to come along with me.

One day, Khokan brought one of his friends, Mizan, who had also heard about my plan. He was keen to join in. Initially, I was reluctant to enlarge the group, fearing that a three-member team would be too big. Furthermore, I was concerned that our potential hosts would not be happy to put up with such a big group of tourists. However, both Khokan and Mizan persuaded me, and thus Mizan became a new group member. However, I was shocked when, one day, Khokan told me that Mizan did not know how to ride a bike. 'You must be joking! A person who doesn't know how to ride a bike wishes to go on a world tour by bicycle?'

Mizan apologised but argued that he was physically fit enough to undertake the tour. He insisted that he could learn to ride a bike very quickly. After Subir managed to find him a bicycle, I started to coach Mizan on how to ride it. After half an hour, Mizan stopped and said, 'Jamal Bhai, it is too embarrassing to learn how to ride a bike during the daytime. The onlookers laugh at me when I fall. Can I practice in the evening, after dark? I told him he should learn and practice day and night if he was serious about going on the tour. Unhappy but undaunted, Mizan gave it his best shot and quickly got the hang of it. He was so excited about the new skill that he practised at every spare moment.

I told Mizan and Khokan that, back in Dhaka, I used to make frequent day trips by bicycle and had always been involved in various physical activities. Even in Agartala, I was trying to keep myself physically fit. I often went jogging in the early morning when the streets were empty. Mizan and Khokan agreed to practice, riding the same bike in rotation every day for a few hours. I also asked them to jog regularly in the early morning and do physical exercise. I warned them they could not go on the tour unless they were physically fit.

Mr Majumdar, the chairperson of the Agartala Congress Committee, tried his best to help us, but after a few days, he gave us bad news. He told us that arranging the international cycle tour from Agartala was impossible. So we had no option but to travel to Kolkata or Delhi to obtain the necessary documents.

Mr Santipada Chowdhury, the trade unionist, informed us that there was no train from Agartala to Kolkata. He suggested that the best thing would be to travel to Dharmanagar, in the northern part of Tripura state, about one hundred miles away from Agartala, where we could catch a train to Kolkata. Mr Chowdhury advised us not to travel by bus, as it would be extremely crowded and take a long time. For this reason, it would be better to travel by truck or lorry. He kindly arranged for our travelling and other expenses to Kolkata.

My stay in Agartala was relatively brief. However, this place had a heart-stirring effect on me. My grandparents did not move to East Pakistan immediately after the partition;

they stayed in Agartala for a few years. I remember visiting them in Agartala when I was a little child. I did not remember anything in particular about this place, but my hazy memories of my grandparents' house gave me warm feelings. However, my experience of Agartala in 1971 will remain memorable for a long time.

Agartala seemed a rather suburban place compared to Dhaka City, where I grew up. The town was sparsely populated and a pleasant place with a fascinating history. All the houses had attractive colourful flower gardens. The most striking thing to me was the sound of music coming from most homes when the children practice music in the early morning. Jogging along the empty streets in the early morning, I would enjoy varieties of music coming from different houses. The scent of freshly bloomed beautiful flowers from the front gardens of each house made my jogging the most enjoyable time of the day. In the evening, everybody dressed as if they were in a fashion show. The girls and women wore make-up and decorated their hair with fresh flowers. The men wore their best outfits. Everybody looked so happy. I felt it was an idyllic society. With this impression of this place, naturally, I felt sad when I had to leave the city so soon.

THREE

Agartala to Kolkata

Tripura is composed of hilly terrain. The route from Agartala to Dharmanagar passes through the hinterlands of Tripura, and the entire way was full of unequalled natural splendour. While I enjoyed the breathtaking natural views, I was more than a little concerned, noticing that the speeding lorry was traversing a relatively narrow road without any railings or protection. I looked out apprehensively at the sight of long, deep valleys with unnervingly steep sides. Often I had to close my eyes and say my last prayer, fearing that if the lorry skidded, there would be a fatal accident. Instead, I focused on the enigmatic hills and the lush green rainforests, trying to ignore the intimidating fall towards the exotic rivers below. However frightening, this was the most adventurous journey I will never forget.

The route from Agartala to Dharmanagar by road was undoubtedly one of the most hair-raising journeys I had ever experienced. However, when we got off the lorry at Dharmanagar, we were relieved to have survived a frightening experience.

We bought some snacks and bananas at the bus station and rushed to the rail station to catch the train to Guwahati, the capital of Assam. Once we settled down on the train, we prepared for a relaxed and enjoyable train journey. We were not disappointed. First of all, we were surprised to notice two additional engines attached to the long train; one in the middle and one at the back. We realised that, like Tripura, Assam also was going to be a hilly region, and without more than one engine, the train would not be able to make it up the slopes. When we approached Guwahati, it was well into the evening, and everything got pretty dark. Suddenly we were struck by the ultra-bright lights from somewhere not far from the railway track. When we got closer to that spot, the intensity of the light increased, but it puzzled us not to see any buildings or structures which these bright lights were supposed to protect. What was, then, the purpose of lighting a large empty area? When I discussed this with Khokan and Mizan, someone overheard me. He explained that the site was a coal mine and was always under guard.

We stayed overnight in Guwahati and, the following morning, got on the train for the long journey to Kolkata.

When we left Assam and entered West Bengal, the countryside appeared very similar to Bangladesh. However, the charm of the train journey faded after a while. In those days (the 1970s), there were no comfortable seats on the train, and the noisy atmosphere was not ideal for a long trip. The route was much longer than we had expected. The scenery became monotonous. We hoped our journey from Assam to Kolkata would end soon.

From Agartala, we circled the whole of Bangladesh to reach Kolkata, west of Bangladesh, via Tripura and Assam.

It would have been a short and enjoyable journey if we could have travelled to Kolkata straight through Bangladesh. However, we would have missed Agartala's scenic natural beauty and parts of Assam.

FOUR

Kolkata

For many people, Kolkata is a magical and exciting city. However, for Bangladeshis, it has a different and unique attraction. Is it because of the similarity of culture, literature, history or something else? None of us could put our finger on any particular reason. Although I had never been to Kolkata, I had heard much about the city. The names of most of the roads and streets were familiar to us because we had watched so many Bengali movies made in Kolkata. Moreover, we learnt about life in Kolkata from books/novels/magazines, newspapers etc.

Once we entered Kolkata, I felt as if I had previously lived in this city. It was like a reincarnation. Kolkata appeared even more intriguing in real life than in my imagination. The more we explored the town, the more we became intensely attracted to this famous cultural spot. Kolkata has a history like no other.

Coming from Dhaka, we should have been lost in a big city like Kolkata. However, everybody was so helpful and cooperative that in no time, we reached the famous refugee camp for the freedom fighters, located in the heart of Kolkata.

The refugee camp was in a big building called the Karnani Estate near Park Circus. The Bangladesh Mission and the Bangladesh Government in Exile were within walking distance from the refugee camp. When we entered the camp, we forgot that we were refugees and freedom fighters. We felt like we had entered a holiday camp.

We stayed on the first floor in a vast open room that looked like a big gym. We were given some bedding to make our beds on the floor. We learned that everybody was waiting to get a place in one of the training camps.

Soon after settling, I contacted people who could help us arrange our cycle tour. Wasting no time, I went to the Bangladesh mission at 9 Circus Avenue and met the Third Secretary, Mr Anwarul Karim Chowdhury. Anwar bhai was the most energetic and capable person in the Mission. He helped us from the moment he met us. First, he heard about the project. Then he considered it an excellent idea. Next, he advised us how to go about it step by step. Anwar bhai also advised us to see officials at the Provisional Government of Bangladesh in exile.

In the Exile Government office, we met Barrister Moudud Ahmed, who worked in the Provisional Government of Bangladesh in Kolkata in the External Publicity Division. Moudud bhai thought it was a splendid idea to go on a world tour by bicycle to strengthen support from other countries for the cause of Bangladesh. He assured us that he would do everything necessary to help us with the project.

One day a young man staying at the same refugee camp approached me. He introduced himself as Babul and took me aside. After a little hesitation, he told me that he knew I was organising a cycle world tour and was keen to join the group.

He was a student at Dhaka University. I guessed that Mizan or Khokan had let the cat out of the bag. I explained to Babul that there were already three of us, and I was reluctant to enlarge the group and gave him my reasons. However, Babul would not give up and tried to convince me by saying how useful a member he could be for the team. He mentioned that his uncle's friend was a prominent businessman in Kolkata, and he could pull in lots of financial and other help from the Kolkata business community.

When Babul realised I was not interested in raising funds for the tour, he changed his tactics. He was persistent with his request and continued, 'Although I am a student, I am also involved with the trade union, and I am the chairperson of the *Sramik League* (Workers' Union) of a Jute mill near my village.' I found Babul very determined and resourceful. Eventually, I became convinced that Babul would be a valuable team member. Although it meant dealing with a larger group, I felt the inclusion of Babul would strengthen the team. So I shook his hand and invited him to join the group. Both Khokan and Mizan were pleased to have Babul in the team.

The more I heard of Anwar Bhai's ability to get things done, the more I felt fortunate to have met him.

Soon after, the Bangladesh Government in exile made the independence declaration, the Pakistan Deputy High Commissioner in India, Mr Hossain Ali, and the third secretary Mr Anwarul Karim Chowdhury, defected from Pakistan and declared their allegiance to Bangladesh Government. However, the most remarkable acts by these two people were that they convinced all the Pakistan Deputy High

Commission staff in Kolkata to defect with them. They also occupied Kolkata's Pakistan High Commission office premises and declared it the Bangladesh Diplomatic Mission. It is them who first hoisted the Bangladesh flag on foreign soil!

One day I found Obaid bhai in the Provisional Government of Bangladesh in exile. Obaid bhai had been an elected member of the National Assembly in the last Pakistan General Elections, the results of which had been ignored by the Pakistan government. I knew Obaid bhai as, at one time, he had lived in our neighbourhood in Dhaka. Obaid bhai liked my idea about the world tour. However, he advised me that we should procure official documents from the Bangladesh Government to go on a world tour. He asked me to provide him with a photo. After a few days, Obaid Bhai gave me an official letter confirming the Bangladesh Government's approval of the cycle tour.

We frequently met with Anwar bhai and Moudud bhai to discuss the project's progress. Finally, one day, Moudud bhai smiled and gave us some news, the best news we could have heard. He told us that the Indian Government had agreed to issue us Indian travel documents so we could go on the world tour. We felt we had leapt over the most challenging hurdle. Shortly afterwards, Anwar Bhai gave us another piece of good news: he had found a sponsor to donate four Hercules cycles for the tour. After obtaining the travel documents, the next step was to get travel visas for the various countries we planned to visit. We then became very busy finalising our route and putting the finishing touches on other minor details of the trip. Finally, Anwar Bhai informed us that he would arrange a press conference to publicise the world tour.

বাংলা দেশ আওয়ামী লীগ

মুজিবনগর

সভাপতি:
শেখ মুজিবুর রহমান

সূত্র

তাং 13.11.1971.

TO WHOM IT MAY CONCERN

Certified that Jamaluddin Md. Hasan has been selected by the members of the Bangladesh Central Students' Action Committee and permission has been given by the Govt. of Peoples' Republic of Bangladesh to go out on a world tour by bicycle with a special aim of steengthening the world opinion in favour of the Great Liberation War of Bangladesh.

Every possible help may please be given to him.

সহ সভাপতি:
সৈয়দ নজরুল ইসলাম
মোঃ মনসুর আলী
খন্দকার মোশতাক আহমদ

(K.M. OBAIDUR RAHMAN) 13.11.71
M.N.A.
Secretary for Social & Cultural Affairs
Bangladesh Awami League.

K. M. Obaidur Rahman
Bangladesh Awami League

সাধারণ সম্পাদক:
তাজউদ্দীন আহমদ

Although we were pretty busy contacting various people and working on our project, I couldn't resist indulging in sightseeing; I wanted to see as much of Kolkata as possible.

During our nearly four-month stay in Kolkata, I spent some of my spare time exploring the city. Despite several attempts, I didn't see everything I wanted; I couldn't visit the Kala Mandir. My biggest regret was my inability to see Shantiniketan ('The Abode of Peace, an educational/cultural institution founded by the Tagore family). It had been top of my wish list and was one of the must-see places in West Bengal. The problem was that Shantiniketan was outside Kolkata, over one hundred and fifty kilometres away. However, the main reason was that I did not have enough money for the travelling expenses.

Although I could not visit Kalamandir and Shantiniketan, I thoroughly enjoyed my stay in Kolkata. Just being there was a pleasure for me. Walking in the various streets, visiting the Howrah Bridge and, spending time in the *Gorer Math*, eating *Telebhaja* from Kolkata's famous street food stalls made me very happy. The other two interesting spots were the Eden Garden Cricket Stadium and the Writers Building. The enormity of the Writers Building was beyond my imagination. Initially, this building housed the clerks of the East India Company. When Kolkata became the capital of British India, the building served as the secretariat of the Bengal State Presidency. I had another reason to be keen to visit this famous building; my father's first job was here.

I felt excited to see the famous Eden Garden Cricket ground. This ground was established in 1864 and is the second-largest cricket stadium in India. Looking around the colossal cricket ground, I thought of the famous cricketers from all over the world who entertained the spectators with their brilliant performances. I particularly remembered the famous umpire, Ganguli. Being influenced by the Pakistani media, we considered him the most partial umpire on the face of the earth. The Pakistani media always led us to believe that Ganguli deliberately took the wrong decisions when giving out to Pakistani batsmen.

During my stay in Kolkata, one of the most enjoyable events I attended was a Puja celebration. I believe it was the *Durga Puja*, the most important and extensive puja in Bengal.

Previously, in Dhaka, I attended a few Saraswati Puja celebrations. Saraswati is the goddess of knowledge, language, music and arts. For Hindu students, this is the most important puja of all. Our Hindu friends would invite us to their Saraswati celebrations. We used to have an enjoyable time in the festive environment, eating delicious food and listening to enchanting music.

However, the puja I attended with my friends in Kolkata was something else. I do not remember how we got the invitation to this particular event; it was at a seemingly wealthy aristocrat's house. From outside, we could hear the music. But, during the week-long puja period, music came from almost everywhere. The whole of Kolkata was in its most festive and joyous mood. As we passed through the front door, we realised this was an extraordinary puja celebration in a remarkable place. I was stunned by the enormity of the building. It had a big inner courtyard with countless rooms on two floors around the inner courtyard, like a palace. The yard was so big and spacious that nearly a hundred people comfortably sat facing a decorated stage where artists performed live music and dance. As soon as new guests arrived, the hosts directed them to climb to the rooftop, where a colourful temporary pavilion had been erected. Mouth-watering food and drink were continuously served on the rooftop by traditionally dressed professional waiters. We were fortunate enough to be given the best seats to view the stage. After about an hour, when we were about to leave, the hosts became concerned and told us that the main dish was going to be served soon and we ought to stay a bit longer! By that time, we had been consuming rich food for nearly an hour; we simply couldn't eat another morsel. So we excused ourselves and reluctantly left the party.

We had nearly finished our preparations and were ready to embark on our trip when we were delighted to hear the unexpected news that Pakistan Army had surrendered to the Bangladesh armed forces and the Indian army. We immediately began celebrating our independence and shelved our plans for the world tour; its purpose seemed redundant.

However, when I thought of all the hard work we had put in, all our efforts would be wasted if we did not find a way to utilise all that we had already achieved. I began to think that we could still go on the tour, but for a different purpose. I began to envisage the tour as a kind of goodwill mission. It would be a true reflection of our gratitude to the people of the world for supporting our cause.

And, of course, it would no longer be appropriate to start the tour from India; we would return to the newly independent Bangladesh and go out into the world to express our profound gratitude to everybody for supporting our liberation war and helping us to win. I discussed my plan with my teammates, Anwar bhai and Moudud bhai, who had been closely involved with us on this project. Everyone agreed that it was a good idea. Anwar bhai said he would contact the sponsor who donated the cycles and explain everything.

We did not want to delay and decided to return to our home country, now free and independent, and now known as Bangladesh.

FIVE

Returning to Independent Bangladesh

As soon as we entered Bangladesh, the sweet smell of freedom in the air made us so happy that we all were in tears. We were overwhelmed by the festive atmosphere everywhere. However, even though we were celebrating our long-sought-after independence, the frightening memories of the massacres throughout 1971 still haunted us.

The Pakistan army brutally murdered three million people during the liberation war. In addition, the military carried out a systematic barbaric act of genocidal rape. As a result, millions of people's hopes and dreams were shattered. We must never forget the sacrifice and suffering of innocent Bangladeshis.

We hurried on towards Dhaka and immediately set out to find our respective parents and close relatives. The anticipation of meeting my close ones was almost too much to bear.

Our house was next to the East Pakistan Rifles (EPR, now the Bangladesh Border Force (BBF)). The whole neighbourhood seemed to have been abandoned and deserted. I was horrified to see the marks and traces of destruction everywhere. Fortunately, I also managed to find three or four families. They had somehow continued to cling to their houses and survive the horror. One of them did not know the whereabouts of my relatives. Another told me they had heard my parents were living somewhere in Azimpur Colony. I kept on praying that I would not face an unpleasant reality. Finally, the third family could give me the address where my parents were staying. I rushed to Azimpur Colony. I was overjoyed to see my parents, brothers and sisters and two other families; one uncle and his family and one cousin and her husband. Altogether fourteen people were cramped together in a three-bedroom apartment. Everybody screamed at the top of their voices, seeing me unexpectedly. It turned out that I was the only unaccounted person in the family. My brother-in-law felt he was in heaven when I gave him a pack of cigarettes that were no longer available in Dhaka!

Although I enjoyed my reunion with my family and relatives and relished living in our now-independent country, I did not set aside my plan for the world tour. Instead, I got in touch with all the team members, reminded them that I did not want to delay and quickly began to make arrangements.

Mizan wanted to drop out of the team. He said, 'Jamal bhai, after so many years of struggle, we have now got our freedom. Now I do not wish to leave the country; I wish to enjoy every moment of freedom.' Mizan was adamant, and I could not persuade him to change his mind.

Mizan dropping out from the team was a big disappointment for me. I was concerned about how others would see us.

There was publicity in the media that a four-member team was about to start the goodwill mission. It might give the wrong impression if we had already lost a member before taking off. Therefore, we had to replace Mizan. Of course, there would be no shortage of enthusiasts wanting to join us, but it would be wise to give some serious thought to the suitability of the prospective fourth member. First, I spoke to Akhtar, one of my childhood friends. He was a professional cyclist, a bodybuilder, tall and robust. It would be a great help for the team to have him as a team member. I, however, had doubts about him agreeing to go out on a world tour, as he was married and they had a newly born daughter, Leeta. However, as soon as I mentioned to him that one of the team members had dropped out and I was looking for a new member, Akhtar jumped to his feet in his excitement and told me, 'Don't look for anyone else. It has been my dream to go on a world tour...'

I said, 'You forget that you are married and...'

'Don't worry. Give me some time to talk to Dilara. But don't offer this opportunity to anyone else until I have spoken to my wife.'

Akhtar rushed home, and it was not long before he returned. He told me that before he approached his wife to discuss going on a world tour, he was nervous. He thought it would be extremely difficult to persuade her to let him leave Dhaka, leaving her and their only child. On the contrary, his wife encouraged Akhtar to participate in this project and said, 'Such an opportunity does not come twice in a lifetime. Participation in this tour will make you feel proud.

If you do not grasp this opportunity, you will regret it all your life; a chance to do something great for the nation.' Dilara bhabi reassured Akhtar, saying, 'I will be OK and will be able to manage Leeta by myself for a year or two.' On the other hand, all his relatives discouraged him from going; they thought it was wrong to leave his wife and child. However, once he knew his wife was happy and encouraged him to participate, Akhtar did not care that his relatives and friends disapproved of the idea.

Once Akhtar had joined the team, we started carrying out the final preparations, ready to set off.

While we were in Kolkata, we realised that we could not enter Europe by land route. At that time, none of the Middle Eastern countries had officially recognised Bangladesh.

Surprisingly, Bangladesh was already beginning to function as a proper country. On 5 February 1972, Bangabandhu realised the importance of the shipping sector, and under the President's Order, he established the Bangladesh Shipping Corporation. Although we did not expect to receive any help from the newly established shipping corporation, we visited them for an informal discussion. We met an officer, Mr Akber Kabir, who was extremely helpful and wrote a letter to the regional director of the Shipping Corporation of India, requesting him to assist us in catching a ship from Bombay to any European port. Mr Kabir was very reassuring, saying that he had every faith in the Shipping Corporation of India in this matter.

National Shipping Corporation

(ESTABLISHED UNDER ORDINANCE NO. IV OF 1963)

Dacca, April 5, 1972.

Dear Mr. Shukla,

4 (Four) students of the Dacca University (1) Mr. Jamal Uddin Md. Hasan, (2) Mr. Anwar Uddin Ahmed, (3) Mr. Mahmud Abdul Quayum and (4) Syed Akhtar Ali are proceeding on a World tour by Bi-cycle on a goodwil mission. They are carrying message from Bangabandhu Sheikh Mujibar Rahman our Prime Minister for the people of the different countries through which they will pass.

As you know to get out of Bangladesh and India one has either to go through Pakistan or through one of the West Asian countries. Under the present situation neither of the course can be undertaken by these adventurous young men. They have no other alternative but to take a boat from Bombay to reach one of the European ports.

I shall be most happy if you could kindly assist them in the matter in consultation with your Head Office in Bombay to reach them to one of the European Ports from Bombay through yourship or any of the sister concern.

Thanking you very much and with the best wishes,

Yours sincerely,

(AKBER KABIR)

Shri P. C. Shukla,
Regional Director,
The Shipping Corporation of India Ltd.,
Calcutta.

Letter from Bangladesh National Shipping Cooperation

When I was working on the original project in Kolkata, my vision for the tour was very different. At that time, I aimed to go out and plead with other nations to support our liberation war. After we were donated four Hercules cycles by Tube Investment of India and the Indian Government issued us international travel documents, we did not think much more about our preparation for the tour, except for obtaining visas for various countries. However, after events on the ground overtook the tour, and the aim was to thank the people of other nations for supporting our cause, my vision of the expedition changed dramatically. As it would be a goodwill mission, we should present ourselves properly. So I started planning for the tour accordingly.

The first thing that came to my mind was to have some small, decorative national flags that we could present to dignitaries in various countries. I also invited Dhaka University and the Bangladesh Sports Federation to sponsor the tour. I visualised us wearing Dhaka University blazers as our formal dress. Also, we should have a distinctive uniform so that people would always recognise our Mission and us. Other essential tasks emerged as I kept thinking of the tour in detail. It was imperative to have a bag/container to carry important articles and documents. I thought of making four unique leather bags, and those could be placed on tailor-made metal baskets fixed at the back of our bikes.

I struggled to cover the cost of getting everything on my shopping list. Then I remembered that, only a few months earlier, while we were in Kolkata, Babul offered to raise funds from Kolkata's business community through his uncle's contacts. At that time, I did not think it was necessary. However, raising funds in the newly independent war-torn country would now be challenging. So I discussed with Babul how to raise funds. Babul reassured me and said, 'Do not worry. Surely, we will be able to raise the required funds in Dhaka.'

First, Babul discussed the issue of raising funds with his uncle, Mr Mukhlesur Rahman, who was the Dhaka City Chamber of Commerce and Industry chair. Babul also made a list of potential donors from his contacts. I then thought of approaching Mr Zohirul Islam, one of the wealthiest men in Bangladesh at that time. For a few days, Babul and I knocked on the doors of potential donors. We received donations from the Dhaka City Chamber of Commerce and Industries, the Bangladesh Jute Board and the Sattar jute mill, where Babul had been the president of the workers union. One movie company, Chayabani Songstha, again from Babul's contact list, promised to donate. A prominent businessman, Mr Zohirul Islam, also contributed to our funds. We did not know then Bangabandhu and our Foreign Minister, Mr Abdus Samad, would also personally contribute to our project.

During the war, Khokan's family house was destroyed, so he became busy sorting out his family's problems. Akhtar became busy ensuring his wife and child would be OK during his absence. He became occupied with arranging everything for his family. However, he volunteered to carry out some specific tasks. Babul often visited his parents outside the city. He would meet me whenever he was in town to discuss the preparations. I devoted my life almost full-time to ensure that we were taking care of everything. Unfortunately, nothing was readily available because the whole country was trying to emerge from the devastation of the war. Akhtar agreed to find a reputable tailor to make our uniforms and made appointments for us to visit the shop to give our measurements. He also volunteered to get the baskets to be fixed at the back of our bikes. I procured tailor-made leather boxes to fit in the grilled baskets. After buying silk materials, I went to Oldtown to find specialised tailors to make decorative flags. I then went to another place in old Dhaka to make carved wooden sticks to be fed through the loops in the flags. Unfortunately, we could not get the Dhaka University blazers. The University advised us to make our own blazers. I went back to Oldtown again to create the monograms for our blazers. Therefore, I was the first to design the Dhaka University Monogram in Bengali! I believe the University later redesigned the monogram professionally.

While getting the essential jobs done, we met Bangabandhu and our Foreign Minister on two or three occasions. Bangabandhu and the Foreign Minister, Abdus Samad, gave us goodwill letters. The Foreign Minister also instructed all the Bangladesh Embassies and High Commission Offices to extend all necessary consular facilities to us.

Bangabandhu was pleased to hear about our plan to go out on a goodwill mission. However, when he learned that we would travel using Indian travel documents, he became annoyed. 'You are citizens of an independent country. You cannot go abroad to represent Bangladesh using refugee passports.' Bangabandhu looked around his advisors and asked, 'How long will it take to get passports?' One advisor responded, 'It may take some time, but they can be issued with Bangladesh travel documents immediately.' Bangabandhu was reassured and smiled with satisfaction.

He told us, 'You must go abroad with Bangladeshi travel documents.' We were so impressed to see Bangabandhu's ability to take note of every little thing!

We were delighted to see Bangabandhu's first Press Secretary, Aminul Haque Badsha (Badsha bhai). I knew Badsha bhai very well. He was a popular student leader and was my older brother's close friend. Badsha bhai was keen to hear our plan in detail. We expressed our wish to start our tour from Bangabandhu's unofficial Residence at 32 Dhanmondi. We chose 7 April 1972 as the departure date. Badsha bhai checked Bangabandhu's diary and told us that it would be possible to see Bangabandhu that morning. Accordingly, we got in touch with the Foreign Minister and informed him of the start date for our cycle world tour from 32 Dhamnodi on 7 April 1972; we would visit him in his Residence, and then we would be on our way to India.

SIX

Entering Kolkata (As tourists)

It was early evening when we reached Kolkata; when we knocked on the doors of the Bangladesh mission, it was after office hours. The caretaker gave us Anwarul Karim bhai's address, which was not far from the Mission. Anwar Bhai was pleased to see us in our uniforms and on our bikes. We were delighted to learn that Anwar Bhai had arranged for us to stay at his Residence during our stay in Kolkata. We informed Anwar Bhai that we did not wish to stay in Kolkata for long and wanted to continue our tour as soon as possible. Anwar Bhai immediately issued a press release, inviting the Indian media to meet us the following day.

বাংলাদেশ প্রেস বিজ্ঞপ্তি

BANGLADESH PRESS RELEASE

Phone 44-5208 / 44-8421

ভারতস্থ বাংলাদেশ হাই কমিশন
৯, সার্কাস এ্যাভিনিউ
কলিকাতা-১৭

be reproduced with or without Acknowledgement)

No. PR-10/72.   APRIL 12, 1972.

BANGLADESH CYCLISTS ON WORLD TOUR

A group of four young Bangladesh cyclists have reached Calcutta on a world tour. They are likely to visit 14 countries of the world. The leader of the group Mr. Jamal Uddin Mohammad Hasan is accompanied by Mr. Anwaruddin Ahmed, Mr. Mahmood Abdul Quayum and Syed Akhtar Ali.

The cyclists' team is carrying with them a message of good wishes from Bangabandhu Sheikh Mujibur Rahman to the people of the countries it will visit.

They will address a press conference tomorrow at 5-00 p.m. at Bangladesh Mission, 9, Circus Avenue, Calcutta - 17.

*****

/SAS/

Because the press conference was at just one day's notice, I feared it would not be well attended. I was wrong. I became excited and, at the same time, nervous, seeing journalists from all the popular newspapers in attendance. All looked interested, expecting to get exciting materials for their newspapers. After Anwar Bhai introduced us to the journalists and explained the purpose of our tour, he invited the journalists to talk to us informally.

With the journalists at the press conference.

In the back of my mind, I had an image of a press conference where journalists give a tough time to their subjects, asking tricky and challenging questions. However, I was very relieved that journalists from the Anandabazar Patrika, the Basumati, Hindustan Standard, and other famous broadsheets eagerly awaited their turn to speak to us individually.

There was no sign of hostility, no interrogation, and no tricky questions. On the contrary, it was friendly and supportive.

After the press conference, we were pleased to see a lot of positive news coverage in popular newspapers. One particular newspaper, The Hindustan Standard, wrote a long, impressive article about us and our goodwill mission. Unlike most other newspapers, this article gave not only the typical information – our names, the purpose of the tour and our planned route – but went deeper. In one section of the extensive article, the journalist wrote,

> *...They carry the good wishes of the newly established Republic of Bangladesh and the Bangabandhu Sheikh Mujibur Rahman, the best passport, into the hearts of the people they intend to visit...*

After giving details of our route, the article continued,

> *...The leader of the group is 23-year-old Jamal Uddin Mohammed Hasan, a dark, lean and keen young man. A postgraduate degree holder in economics, he is a good all-around sportsman. He is accompanied by Anwaruddin Ahmed, a final-year Honours Student in Geography, Mohammed Abdul Quayum, a first-year postgraduate student in International Relations and Syed Akhtar Ali, a college student. Of the lot, the last is almost a professional cyclist. The choice of the members of this expedition is interesting though one is not sure whether the men or organisation behind it had this idea in mind. The economist is correctly the leader because he will control the finances, the geography student will decide the route, the cyclist will make sure that the Indian-made cycles are in good order, and the international relations student will be the spokesman... In another part of the long article, the journalist comments,*
>
> *...Though the intention behind the expedition seems political, the laudable factor is that these lads would like to carry their people's message of goodwill by cycle. The very spirit of adventure, for the hazards of travelling by cycle, are many, makes it a thrilling sport.*

During our short stay in Kolkata, we were fortunate to meet the Chief Minister of West Bengal, Mr Subrata Mukherjee.

The Chief Minister was pleased to meet us and assured us that he would ask the Central Government to help us with our tour.

We also met the Secretary to the Government of West Bengal PWD, Mr P.C. Banerji. Mr Banerji kindly gave us a letter of introduction, requesting that accommodation in bungalows on our way to Delhi be provided free of cost. This was a really useful and helpful addition to our resources.

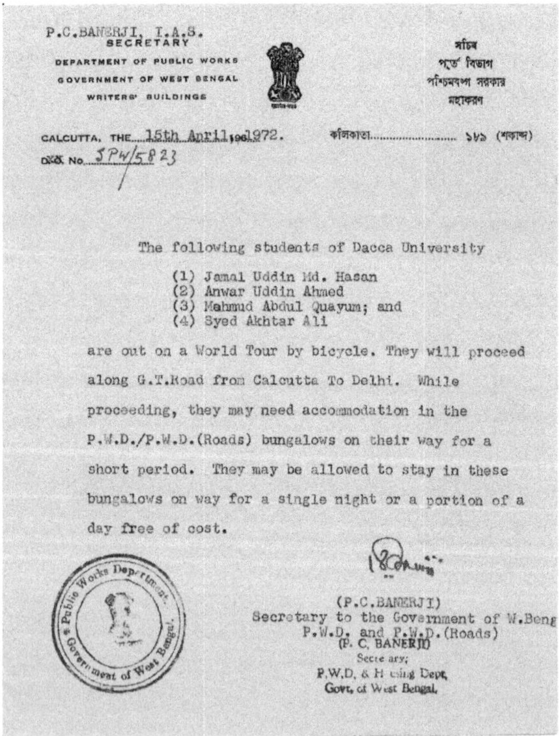
P.C.BANERJI, I.A.S.
SECRETARY
DEPARTMENT OF PUBLIC WORKS
GOVERNMENT OF WEST BENGAL
WRITERS' BUILDINGS

সচিব
পূর্ত বিভাগ
পশ্চিমবঙ্গ সরকার
মহাকরণ

CALCUTTA, THE 15th April, 1972.   কলিকাতা.................... ১৮৯ (শকাব্দ)
D.O. No. SPW/5823

The following students of Dacca University

(1) Jamal Uddin Md. Hasan
(2) Anwar Uddin Ahmed
(3) Mahmud Abdul Quayum; and
(4) Syed Akhtar Ali

are out on a World Tour by bicycle. They will proceed along G.T.Road from Calcutta To Delhi. While proceeding, they may need accommodation in the P.W.D./P.W.D.(Roads) bungalows on their way for a short period. They may be allowed to stay in these bungalows on way for a single night or a portion of a day free of cost.

(P.C.BANERJI)
Secretary to the Government of W.Beng
P.W.D. and P.W.D.(Roads)

(P. C. BANERJI)
Secretary;
P.W.D. & Housing Dept.
Govt. of West Bengal.

Public Works Department ★ Government of West Bengal

SEVEN

Bihar

Soon after we left West Bengal and entered Bihar, we felt we were in a foreign environment. Since early 1971, we have been to Agartala, Assam and Kolkata. However, until then, we had never missed Bangladesh so far as the climate, culture, language, and, most importantly, the food was concerned. Bihar was very different. First of all, the language was foreign to us. Although Hindi is the official language of Bihar, the spoken language here is Hindustani, an everyday mix of Hindi and Urdu. However, there are different dialects in different parts of Bihar. The most popular ones are Bhojpuri, Magahi and Maithili. We understood a little bit of Hindi and Urdu. However, we were not conversant in Hindustani and the other local dialects in Bihar. Besides, the different food and the scorching temperature reminded us that we were in a foreign country for the first time. It was only the end of April. We started anticipating hotter months ahead. We worried that the heat would pose a real threat to us come May and June.

We rode our bikes on the famous Grand Trunk Road, popularly known as GT Road. A sixteenth-century ruler, Sher Shah Suri, built this highway. It is the oldest and longest major road in the Indian subcontinent. It runs roughly

3,670 km (2,280 miles) from Kabul in Afghanistan, passing through Amritsar, Delhi, Allahabad, Bihar, Kolkata, Dhaka and Cox's Bazaar in Bangladesh. In the past, this road was also known as Uttarpath, Sarak-e-Azam, and Badshahi Sarak. Today, India has given parts of the GT road the title of the highway. Some stretches of the GT road are now known as National Highway NH2, NH19, NH91 etc. In Bangladesh, a long stretch of the GT road in Jessore was named Jessore Road, and I have told the story of this stretch of road already.

Although local people started to call this part of the GT Road Jessore Road, it is still the GT Road for the old-timers. It is worth mentioning that on the GT Road from Kabul to Cox's Bazaar, nowhere one can find such a scenic tree-lined smooth road as Jessore Road. This stretch of the road is unique and remarkable.

During the liberation war, the Jessore Road became famous after Allen Ginsberg wrote a poem, *September on Jessore Road*, which described the plight of the refugees as a result of the Pakistan army's brutal attack on innocent Bangladeshis. This emotive poem became famous and attracted people worldwide to condemn Pakistan's atrocities in Bangladesh.

In Bihar, we soon encountered a bigger problem than the heatwave. Babul became ill with a high temperature and stomach problems. We had just passed a small town in Bihar called Dhanbad when we realised that Babul's condition was worsening. One of us went ahead of Babul, and two rode behind him, encouraging him to push forward. We took an early lunch break, hoping Babul would feel better after taking a long rest. However, Babul was pessimistic about recovering so soon. Poor Babul looked very sickly.

In the restaurant, we attracted the attention of our fellow diners because we were in our uniform, all wearing the same coloured shorts and T-Shirts with the same monograms. Some of them must have thought we were insane to ride bikes in the scorching heat. One Sikh gentleman approached us. He introduced himself as Colonel Singh. We thought his real name might have been Karamjit Singh, and he was popularly known as Karnal or Colonel Singh. When he learnt that we were from Bangladesh and on a world tour, he shared his exciting findings with others. He was concerned to hear that Babul was suffering from a high temperature. He advised us that it would be unwise to cycle in this hot temperature, especially when one of us was ill. When he learned that we were planning to visit Gaya, Patna and Varanasi before going to Lucknow and Delhi, he told us that he could give us a lift in his lorry. Unfortunately, he was not heading directly to Patna, but he would pass close to Banaras. Because of Babul's illness, we thought it was wise to accept Mr Singh's offer. Mr Singh advised us to rest, as he was not going out in the heat. It suited us to start the journey in the evening and travel through the twilight so that Babul could take a complete rest.

Accepting this offer of a lift meant we would miss the opportunity of visiting one of the seven holy cities in India. Gaya is a holy city not only for the Hindus, but it is also a revered holy city for Jain and Buddhists. It is believed that Buddha attained enlightenment in this city. This wonderful history marks Gaya as one of the four sacred sites of Buddhism.

Ever since I was a child, I have heard the famous phrase, 'Goya, Kashi, Brindavan'. This phrase was a renowned piece of dialogue for aged Hindu women in movies and novels, expressing the feeling that they had exhausted the desire to live in a materialistic world and were longing to enter into the spiritual and religious life by making the pilgrimage to Goya, Kashi and Brindavan.

EIGHT

Varanasi (Banaras)

We travelled a good part of Bihar in Mr Singh's lorry. The journey was quite enjoyable. Mr Singh's occasional commentaries about the places we passed kept us awake throughout the trip. Only Babul constantly slept throughout the trip, and we tried to sleep on and off whenever Mr Singh took a pause from his commentaries. I was asleep when we crossed Bihar and entered Uttar Pradesh. However, it would have made no difference to me had I been awake!

It was early morning when Mr Singh stopped the lorry, and we realised we had reached our destination. Mr Singh got down and stretched his legs, and we, too, got down slowly. Mr Singh told us that we were just a few miles away from Banaras city centre. He gave us directions and reassured us that it would not take long.

We all got our bikes down.

Mr Singh advised us to take care of ourselves and wished us well. We profoundly thanked him for looking after us since we had met him the previous afternoon. We thanked him for his valuable advice about not riding our bikes in the worst heat of the day. We also thanked him for his hospitality, for paying our restaurant bills at Dumri, and for the refreshments on the long way from Dumri to Banaras.

Having had a complete rest in the lorry, Babul felt slightly better and managed to ride the bike slowly to reach a guest house in Banaras city centre.

The temperature was rising every minute. After a heavy breakfast, we decided to rest for the afternoon before venturing into the heat to explore the famous holy city.

Hindus believe Banaras is the home of Lord Shiva, who, according to them, is the 'god of all gods'. Some Hindus also believe that the holy River Ganges pays its respects to Lord Shiva by changing the direction in which it flows. It literally changes its direction of flow from the south to the north to pass Banaras.

Banaras is the holiest of all the holy cities in India. Gautama Buddha developed Buddhism in nearby Saranath and gave his first sermon there. As well as Hindus, Banaras is also a holy place for pilgrimage for Jain followers, because many *Tirthankaras* were born in Banaras. Tirthankaras are the gods of the Jain religion; they are born as human beings, but through meditation, they attain a state of perfection and enlightenment. Banaras has over three thousand Hindu religious places, over one thousand Muslim holy places, twelve Churches, nine Buddhist shrines, three Jain Temples and three Gurdwaras. According to Hindu legend, Banaras is the oldest city in the world, and Kashi Vishwanath is the most important temple out of all Hindu temples in the world.

After taking a rest, we set out to explore the holy city. First, we headed towards the Kashi Vishwanath temple, the main tourist attraction of Banaras. The temple was not far. We decided to walk so that we could see the town. It did not take long to reach one of the most sacred places for all Hindus in India and worldwide. Hindus are expected to make a pilgrimage to the Kashi Vishwanath temple at least once in their lifetime.

I had never undertaken a pilgrimage, although I had visited one historical mosque in the past. I remember my experience inside the mosque as quiet and peaceful. I also remember when I first entered a library; I felt the same quietness and peace. In a holy place, the devotees go there to seek peace. Similarly, knowledge-seekers go to a library to seek knowledge. In both settings, people reach their highest levels of concentration.

People who visit the famous Kashi temple are mostly pilgrims from various places, including from outside India. In the past, a pilgrimage meant walking to the holy site, which often took days, weeks or months. The long journey itself came to be part of the act of pilgrimage. This journey prepares the mind for the experience of the holy place. Today, people make the pilgrimage by many different modes of transport, although some still prefer to make the old style of pilgrimage, arriving at the holy place on foot. Once they reach the sacred place, they become overwhelmed by the spiritual atmosphere, and the gathering of devotees, all of them moved by an inexplicable emotion.

Once we entered the temple compound, I felt something quite strange and unusual. I found the temple compound so quiet and peaceful as if some invisible heavenly power shielded the place from the chaos outside. The devotees and the tourists, like us, were calm as if we were in a different world; as if we all were fully anaesthetised, having no pain in our body and mind, no sign of anxiety; as if people were there to take a break from the things that afflicted their troubled and tired souls. Most importantly, there was no sign of boasting about one's wealth, authority and power. Instead, all appeared to be humble, collectively surrendering to the higher spiritual power.

I realised that one does not have to belong to a particular religion – or any religion – to appreciate being in a holy place. Because people at a sacred place are always on their best behaviour, the atmosphere is quite different from other sites. It seems that one's mental state is elevated from ordinary to extraordinary. However, we did not enter the temple, thinking that, as we were not Hindus, it might not be appropriate for us to do so.

We were all moved by our visit. So we decided to visit the other famous temple in Banaras, the Sarnath Temple, the following day.

We decided to walk back along the river bank. We saw hundreds of people, men and women of all ages, bathing in the River Ganges, the holy river to all Hindus. The water did not look clean to us; it appeared rather dirty. There were several ghats on the riverbank. Some were meant for bathing, and others for cremation. For devout Hindus, a ceremonial dip in the holy water of the Ganges in Banaras is believed to purify the soul and wash away all sins. The polluted water, where the ashes from cremation are frequently seen floating around, did not deter them from dipping their hands in and throwing the dirty water on their heads.

The Hindus believe that to be cremated in Banaras by the River Ganges and have one's ashes scattered in the holy water of the Ganges guarantees that their soul will be transported to heaven, bypassing the cycle of rebirth. For this reason, there are many designated ghats along the river. First, the dead body is dipped in the holy water; then, it is covered with cotton and ghee and placed upon the funeral pyre, which is then set on fire.

We learned that a boat ride on the Ganges in the early morning was very pleasant and enjoyable. So we decided to give it a go. We got up quite early and headed towards the river the next day. Although it was early in the morning, hundreds of people were already bathing in the river. We also noticed the funeral pyres were still burning. Someone told us that the cremation continues twenty-four hours a day! The temperature in the early morning in Banaras was so pleasant we almost forgot that it would rise to the point of discomfort in only a few hours.

After lunch, we set off for the Sarnath Temple, one of the holiest places for Buddhists. There were facilities for anyone, Buddhists or not, to go inside the temple and view the galleries of pictures depicting Gautama Buddha's life and work. The legendary collection dates back to ancient times. Seeing the Dhamek Stupa, we tried to imagine the time, back in the fifth or sixth century BC, when the Buddha sat precisely on that spot and gave his first sermon. It was not difficult to travel to the past. I just closed my eyes and felt the living presence of the Buddha.

When we were planning to return to the guesthouse,

all four of us were startled to hear someone talking to us in Bengali, 'You people must be from Bangladesh!' We were surprised to discover that the person talking to us was a Swami, in his special outfit. He looked more surprised than us, hearing our Bangladeshi accents.

Since we had left West Bengal, we had not heard anyone speaking Bengali. However, the Swamiji was so pleased to have met us that he introduced us to some of his friends and fellow pilgrims. After he heard about the purpose of our world tour, he and his friends became so interested in us that they invited us to a restaurant for lunch so that we could continue our discussion about the liberation war.

We talked about our struggle in the liberation war and concluded that good wishes from people worldwide had washed away all our sufferings. Therefore, we were happy and wanted to thank everybody for their good wishes.

I changed the subject and asked Swamiji to tell us about the importance of Banaras for the Hindu religion.

Swamiji was pleased that we were keen to know about the Hindu religion. He explained that Kashi Vishwanath Temple is the most important Hindu temple. Lord Shiva founded this temple. Swamiji concluded, 'We believe Banaras this is the oldest city on earth.' I asked Swamiji to explain the phrase, 'Goya, Kashi, Vrindavan'.

Swamiji smiled and was pleased to explain that the order of importance of these three holy places should have been Kashi, Vrindavan, and Goya. However, from Bengal, the distance to Goya is the shortest, and Vrindavan is the longest.

For this reason, the phrase has become Goya, the nearest, Kashi in the middle and Vrindavan as the last destination.

Swamiji explained many other exciting events from Hindu mythology in such a convincing way that I felt myth and belief were interwoven so profoundly that any different view, whether logical or not, could not intrude on the devotees' beliefs. I also felt that most of us, from whatever educational, religious or social backgrounds we come from, hold specific beliefs about life, destiny and the future. When we say, 'It was not to be,' we are not talking scientifically; we are expressing our beliefs. To some extent, we can be fatalists when we do not know the answers or have the strength and ability to divert our minds to explore the facts.

In visiting the holy city, we felt we had encountered a new experience that was very important to us.

The next day, on our way to Lucknow, we decided to visit the biggest Hindu University in the world. The entrance looked like the portal to a museum. We got off our bikes and strolled towards the main compound.

A few students approached us, realising that we were not from the University. They came to us to ask if we needed any help. We explained that we were tourists from Bangladesh and did not wish to see anything in particular. We just came to see the University. Looking at the leather box at the back of our bikes where it was written'World Tourist Bangladesh, they realised we were on a world tour. They happily gave us a guided tour of the University. They asked us about the liberation war and wondered how we could defeat the mighty Pakistan army.

We were surprised to see the enormity of the university compound. We found out that the University had two campuses, sixteen faculties and one hundred and forty departments. After walking for about half an hour on the campus, we realised that it would take much longer to see the full extent of it. We, therefore, decided to leave the Hindu University and say goodbye to the students.

NINE

Lucknow

We decided to pedal non-stop to Joanpur. In Joanpur, we visited a famous TD college. We were impressed by the gorgeous main entrance and the premises. However, we realised it was a reasonably new building by India's standards. Unlike other establishments that have existed for centuries, it was founded relatively recently, in 1914, by Mr Tilak Dhari Singh, the first graduate in the district of Joanpur.

Seeing the written text on the leather boxes, 'World Tourist, Bangladesh', some students approached us and began chatting. They wanted to know about the liberation war and how we made the mighty Pakistan army surrender to us. The students were so hospitable that they invited us to stay in their hostel instead of finding a guesthouse. Unfortunately, as we were concerned about lagging with our schedule, we had to decline their invitation.

Leaving TD College, we rode until the evening and stopped for the night at Sultanpur. Our destination, Lucknow, was still one hundred and fifty kilometres away. We again stopped for an overnight stay at Haidergarh, some fifty kilometres from Lucknow.

Reaching Lucknow, we did not need to look for a guesthouse or a hotel for our short stay. While in Kolkata, we were invited by Mr Ramesh Roy for dinner. As Mr Roy was a friend of Babul's *mama* (uncle), we started to call him Ramesh Mama. At the dinner table, Ramesh mama told us that his younger brother, Arun Roy, lived in Lucknow. He wrote down Arun Roy's address and said that his brother would be pleased if we stayed with him during our stay in Lucknow. He also told us that he would write to him about us.

Before going to Arun mama's house, we cycled around Lucknow to see the tourist attractions. We were pleasantly surprised to see the beautiful city, which looked like a museum full of beautiful architecture, with impressive monuments everywhere.

We knocked on Arun mama's front door just before it got dark. It turned out that Arun mama, his wife, and their three children had been eagerly waiting to receive us since the previous day.

Arun mama and the whole family, māmi, their three children and his mother-in-law, were delighted to welcome us as their guests. They had already made all the necessary arrangements for us to stay with them in their big house.

Arun mama's family reminded us of a typical Bengali joint/extended family, consisting of their children, mother-in-law, an uncle and a few nephews. Instantly mama, māmi and everybody in the house became so friendly with us that we felt as if we had known each other for a long time. Everybody was excited about having us in their home and started asking us questions.

Finally, Māmi, with a smile, told us, 'You have cycled all day. You must be tired and hungry. Please freshen up first and then we'll continue the discussion at the dinner table.' Then she asked one of her children to show us the bathroom.

Once we settled down at the dining table, we were pleasantly surprised to see the mouth-watering dishes. We were so hungry that we couldn't wait to eat. We had not eaten any Bengali dishes since leaving Kolkata. So we started serving ourselves and tucked in as if we had never had such delicious food before. We paused to thank Māmi and said, 'Since we left Kolkata, we have been dying for delicious Bengali dishes like these.' While we were trying every dish, the children kept us busy, asking us questions about the liberation war. Mama and Māmi attempted to control the children. 'Can you stop asking too many questions? Let them eat first. You have the whole night to listen to the interesting stories.'

Although we enjoyed describing our experiences to everybody, we felt too tired to stay awake. After cycling all day and having a heavy dinner, we wished to find our beds as soon as possible. Mama rescued us from the children and showed us two rooms with two beds in each room. With a smile, mama said, 'If you wish, you could choose a better place to sleep.' We protested, 'These rooms are fine for us...' However, mama insisted we see the alternative place and asked us to follow him. Mama led us to the rooftop. He said that in Lucknow, most people with access to a rooftop slept on the roof on a 'Khatia' (or *Charpai, a* light, portable four-legged bed made of rope net on a wooden frame). Mama explained that sleeping in the bedrooms in the summer is uncomfortable because of the high temperatures. We noticed that many people on other rooftops had settled on their Khatia. Mama explained, 'It is cool up here, and you will be able to sleep comfortably.'

Arun Mama and mami on their rooftop

With Arun Mama Mmi and her mother

With Arun Mama's extended family members

We realised the original occupiers of these khatia were giving them up for us. We were happy to experience sleeping under the sky in the cool breeze rather than suffocating in a stuffy room. Māmi gave us four blankets and warned, 'In the early morning, you will feel cold, so keep these blankets in case.'

It was lovely sleeping under the star-studded sky. It was a good job that mama suggested we sleep on the rooftop. We had a very sound sleep. Mami was right about the morning; when we felt cold, we pulled out the blankets to cover ourselves.

There were so many things to see in Lucknow. So we decided that our top priority would be to visit the Chief Minister and the Governor of Lucknow and then devote our time to visiting the famous tourist attractions.

We were extremely fortunate to see the Chief Minister and the Governor without prior appointments. Both of them engaged in a detailed discussion about the liberation war and praised us for our determination to become independent. They praised the Bangladeshi people for our decision to move towards secularism and socialism and wished us success on our world tour. We expressed our gratitude for India's support in our struggle, without which it would have taken us a long time to realise our freedom.

After seeing the Chief Minister, we went to see the Governor of Lucknow. The Governor was extremely busy with his daily duties. However, he managed to have a detailed discussion with us.

After the discussion, when we were about to leave, the Governor invited us to attend his daughter's wedding that evening. We thanked him profoundly for the invitation. But unfortunately, we could not accept the invitation because we had a prior engagement with Arun mama to visit the Bengali Association, a social club, in Lucknow that evening.

We had a lovely time at the Bengali Association Social club. It was a typical Bengali club that served as a meeting place for the Bengali people, and gossiping was the main attraction.

After finishing the essential tasks, we set off sightseeing in the city. Like Kolkata, Lucknow is another famous cultural spot in India. Ever since we were young, we had heard stories about Uttar Pradesh as a distinguished region in India. We heard that the people of Uttar Pradesh, particularly Lucknow, were cultured, eloquent and sophisticated in their manners, behaviour and appearance. The people of Lucknow were enlightened, and anybody could recognise them as persons of good taste for food and arts.

GOVERNOR
UTTAR PRADESH

RAJ BHAVAN
LUCKNOW

April 30, 1972.

I was very happy to meet Messrs Jamal Uddin Mohd. Hasan, Anwar Uddin Ahmed, Mahmud Abdul Qayum and Syed Akhtar Ali, students of the Dacca University and members of the historic 'Mukti Bahini', today. They apprised me of the various events during their Freedom Struggle and told me that they are on a goodwill mission to various countries of the world. I am sure, they will be given a roaring welcome wherever they go - as messengers of Freedom, Secularism and Socialism.

I wish them every success in their venture.

B. Gopala Reddi

(B. Gopala Reddi)

Lucknow, the capital of Uttar Pradesh, was famously known as the city of Nawabs. It has a glorious history. The

Nawabs promoted and sponsored arts, poetry, music, songs and dance. As a result, the people of Lucknow became a distinct class of people in India. Long before the Nawabs, this region was already famous for its culture and music for many years. It produced many legendary musicians. Amir Khasrau, universally known as the father of Indian classical music, was born here in 1253. Amir Khasru was a famous poet who also created the foundations of Indian classical music.

Many composers and poets thrived under the lavish patronage of the Nawab rulers. All the Nawabs followed the ancient customs of the region, particularly the last Nawab, Wajid Ali Shah, who was a poet, a playwright, a dancer and a fabulous arts patron. He is widely credited with the revival of Kathak as a primary form of classical Indian dance. Lucknow is also famous for holding poetic events. Poets from all over the world visit Lucknow to participate in these poetic events and festivals. Lucknow is like Florence in Italy and Sarajevo in the Balkan states. It has always been rich in developing and maintaining its culture to the highest standard.

The cultural tradition continued even after the Nawabs left the scene. More recent notables from arts and culture include Naushad Ali, undoubtedly the best Indian motion picture composer and music director. He is mainly known for popularising the use of classical music in films. The Bollywood film industry owes a debt to Naushad for making Hindi films so popular worldwide. Besides Naushad Ali, another famous singer, Talat Mahmood, was born here. And what a coincidence that one of the legendary British singers, Sir Cliff Richard, was also born in Lucknow.

Besides literature, music and arts, Lucknow also developed one of the most famous Indian dishes, Biryani. Although some people claim that the Mughals brought this dish from Persia, many historians believe that, long before the Mughals came to India, the Turk-Mongol conqueror, Taimur, brought Biryani to India in the year 1398. The Nawabs appreciated this delicacy, and they extensively developed this dish in Lucknow. Because of the Nawabs of Lucknow, Biryani became one of the most popular Indian dishes in the region and beyond.

The architecture of the buildings and memorials reminded us of the Muslim influence everywhere. All the Nawabs, particularly the fourth Nawab, Asaf Ud Daula, created significant landmarks in Lucknow. When a famine struck Uttar Pradesh, the Nawab decided to provide jobs to the poor and build the Bara Imambara, a unique building. He also created the Rumi Darwaza, an imposing gateway. He provided the poor with food and jobs and made an unforgettable impression on Lucknow's architecture and culture.

Lucknow's contribution to Indian styles of dress and its unique mode of embroidery, called Chiskankari, is famous all over India.

Until we visited the Bara Imambara, we were under the impression that it was a famous mosque. We then found out it was a place for believers to assemble and mourn Imam Hossain during the month of Muharram. We also found out that the structure of Bara Imambara is unique in India. The colossal structure is balanced without any pillars and beams. The roof rests on a network of corridors, arched doors and windows.

Entering the Bara Imambara

The network of corridors makes it a fantastic maze, with identical doorways and staircases. People rely on professional guides to venture into the labyrinth as there is a good chance of getting lost.

On the rooftop of Bara Imambara

The maze has fantastic acoustics. A person whispering at one end can be heard at the other end. Even the light from one of the balconies can be seen from the other side. The most interesting feature of the Bara Imambara is that there is a staircase leading to an underground pond. No wonder the Bara Imambara has always n a must-see tourist attraction for anyone visiting Lucknow. Besides this unique engineering feature, Bara Imambara has many interesting facts and stories.

One interesting legend is that there are several tunnels underneath the Bara Imambara. These tunnels lead to Delhi, Faizabad, Allahabad and the Gomti River. However, the most exciting tale, which seems very unlikely, is that the maze of corridors was meant for the Nawab's wife to play hide and seek with her friends!

We heard about the British Residency in Lucknow, which was created for the British Resident General. During the 1857 mutiny, this complex was subjected to a siege by the rebels. Nearly 2,000 British lost their lives in the siege, including the General. Finally, the surviving British were evacuated, but the Residency was abandoned. Looking at the ruins, one can imagine the past glorious image of this enormous complex. Although the place did not have a happy ending, it still impresses the visitors with its sombre appearance and the graveyard for the people who died during the siege, with touching epitaphs engraved on the gravestones. The British Residency of Lucknow has become a famous historical landmark. The ruins of the Residence now serve as a tourist attraction.

In the evening, mama took us to the Bengali Club & Youngmen's Association in Lucknow. As soon as we entered the crowded club, we felt at home. The members warmly welcomed us. They got involved in a long conversation about our experience of the liberation war. Everybody was proud of us, and we took the opportunity to express our gratitude to them. We enjoyed our time at the Youngmen's Association so much that we stopped feeling bad for missing the Governor's wedding.

In hindsight, I am surprised and pleased that we managed to do many things in such a short stay in Lucknow – just two days and three nights.

TEN

Kanpur

After two hectic days of running around and visiting many tourist spots in Lucknow, we felt exhausted. So we decided to have a late breakfast before setting off for Kanpur, our next destination. When Mami suggested that we leave after lunch, we readily agreed.

Soon after we got out of Lucknow and entered the Kanpur region, it got dark. We started to look for a guest house for the night. There were not that many people I could ask for help. Suddenly seeing the light coming out from a building, we approached, hoping to get some information about the nearest guest house. When we got closer to the building, we realised it was a police station. We found the name of the place was Ajgain. We went inside the police station to ask for information. The police officers were surprised to see four cyclists walking into their office in uniforms at that time of the day. We explained that we were not in trouble but were only looking for directions. When they realised that we were from Bangladesh and were out on a world tour, they immediately engaged in a conversation.

There were four of them on duty, and all of them forgot what we were looking for, but became busy asking us question after question about our liberation war. Finally, we explained that it would have taken many years to defeat Pakistan without international support, particularly from India. Therefore, we thought it was our duty to express our gratitude to the world.

It was getting late. So we modestly reminded them that we were looking for a guest house for the night. They looked at each other, and then one of them apologetically said there was no guesthouse in that area. However, they would be more than happy to arrange some accommodation for us for the night at the police station! We were in a dilemma as to whether we should accept their offer. The police officers sensed that we were not too keen to sleep in the police station. One of them told us there was a big room at the back and assured us that, although it would not be comfortable, we would be all right for one night. As we had no alternative, we agreed. The boss then asked another officer to arrange for our dinner.

They continued with the questions about the liberation war at the dinner table and expressed their happiness that it was over. The officers then asked us many questions about our cycle tour, the places we had already been to, other places in India and what other countries we would be travelling to. Finally, the youngest of the four officers said, 'I envy you people. How lucky you are travelling the world to represent your country, and I will be stuck in this place forever!' We tried to encourage him to be optimistic about the future.

We were so pleased to receive VIP treatment from these friendly people. Because of their sincerity and taking good care of us, everything turned out to be very pleasant. The food tasted delicious, and the beds seemed heavenly and comfortable.

We found a hot breakfast waiting for us in the morning. We profoundly thanked the officers for looking after us so well. Soon after breakfast, we set off for Kanpur Town centre.

Until the British defeated Nawab Shuja-ud-Daula and took over Kanpur in 1765, this area was a backward and insignificant region. However, since the British and European business people established themselves in Kanpur, it gradually became an industrial town. As a result, it soon became one of India's leading centres of the industrial revolution and popularly became known as the Manchester of the East.

We did not make a detour on our way to Delhi and visit Kanpur for its industrial history, but for another important reason. We wanted to meet the Tube Investment of India manager, Mr Mehta, who had kindly donated four cycles for the tour. We had met him before when he presented the cycles at the Bangladesh Mission in Kolkata at a press conference.

Mr Mehta was pleased to meet us again. He was delighted to know that the bicycles were behaving fine and we had had no trouble. We collected our mail from relatives who sent care of Tube Investment. Mr Mehta wished us good luck and asked us to inform him about our tour.

Leaving the Tube Investment office, while we were touring the city, we attracted a group of young people, most of whom were students. They informed us that the Dhaka University hockey team would be playing a friendly match against Kanpur University that evening. Naturally, we immediately decided to watch this match. We were also expecting to meet some friends.

We met the Dhaka University team before the match started. As we expected, we met the Bangladesh hockey star Ibrahim Saber, the only hockey player from East Pakistan to be included in the Pakistan National team to play in the Barcelona Olympics. They were excited about meeting us unexpectedly and commented, 'How lucky we are to find you people here to support us in the game!'

When the match started, we realised that the Dhaka University team did not need the support of the four of us; they had the majority of the spectators in the stadium supporting them and screaming with excitement whenever they did well. The true meaning of a friendly game!

ELEVEN

Delhi

Entering New Delhi, we were amazed by seeing the vast open spaces. We did not feel like a fish out of water. On the contrary, we felt we had been picked out of the fishbowl and thrown into the ocean! Everything appeared different to us. We, however, later experienced the congested Old Delhi, which felt much more like being at home.

In some respects, the success of our world tour depended heavily on our activities in New Delhi. So we headed towards the Bangladesh High Commission to meet His Excellency Dr A R Mallick, the first Bangladesh Ambassador to India, without wasting time. HE Mallick was the VC of Chittagong University. He was not only renowned as an academic but also for his active involvement in the Bangladesh liberation movement.

His Excellency Mallick was pleased to receive us. He was enthusiastic to know about our experience so far and congratulated us for organising this world tour for such a noble purpose.

He knew we wanted to meet the Indian Prime Minister, Indira Gandhi. He warned us that getting an appointment may take some, but he would do his best for us. While talking to us, he sent for Mr Ganguly.

Mr Ganguly did not wait for His Excellency Mallick to introduce us to him. He was excited to see us and said, 'I have seen you people in the papers. I am so proud of you. Well done!'

His Excellency Mallik asked Mr Ganguly to arrange a place for us to stay for a few days. Excited, Mr Ganguly said, 'It will be my pleasure to find a suitable place for these heroes in New Delhi.'

We started to call him Ganguly'da. 'Da' is an abbreviation of 'Dada' (older brother in West Bengal). Ganguly'da drove his car slowly and asked us to follow him on our bikes. I wondered how he was going to find accommodation. Suddenly he stopped in front of a restaurant and said, 'You people must be hungry.' He took out some cash from his pocket, and as he gave us the money, he said, 'I will make a few phone calls and get back before you finish your lunch.' Before he left, he asked one of the restaurant workers to keep our bikes in a secure place.

As promised, he returned before we finished our lunch. He looked cheerful and excited. 'I have found one of the best places for you. You will love this place and will enjoy your stay there.' He gave us the address and directions to reach there and said, 'Your host is waiting for you. I will meet you there to help you settle down.'

The place he found for us was a hostel, and we were delighted to realise that it was not an ordinary hostel but a hostel for MPs located in the centre of New Delhi!

Gaguly'da reached the hostel before us. He introduced us to Mr Sheel Bhadra Yajee. Mr Yajee warmly welcomed us, and then he became busy making us feel at home. The MP hostel looked like a very decent hotel. Mr Yajee asked us to take seats in the lobby and asked a waiter to bring some cold drinks and to organise our accommodation.

We found Mr Yajee a true patriot and a very dedicated politician. He had recently retired from active politics but had lingered on with political activities like a full-timer. While he was talking to us, he received some telephone calls. Before starting his conversation, he would say 'Jay Hind' first and end the conversation by using the same slogan. We never heard him say 'hello' or 'bye'. The more we knew about Mr Yajee, the more we liked him. I noticed he closely resembled one of my favourite West Bengal film actors, Pahari Sanyal. I also thought his character was close to Pahari Sanyal. In no time, Mr Yajee became very friendly with us. He became so close to us that he started making jokes with us. I still remember how he once teased us, 'You Bengali people eat everything. You eat rice, eat medicine, you eat water and even cigarettes! You do not drink or smoke. You eat everything!'

We later learned that he was an activist of the 'Kishan' Movement and a close associate of Netajee Subash Chandra Bose. No wonder he would say 'Jay Hind' all the time, as Netaji Subash Chandra Bose invented this famous slogan. Mr Yajee had been arrested by the British Raj many times. To avoid arrest, he often went underground. In 1947 he was in prison, serving an eight-month sentence because he was in touch with Netaji Subash Bose. He escaped jail on 15 August 1947, when India became independent.

After Congress adopted its socialist manifesto, Nehru

persuaded him to join Congress. Since joining the Congress, he had been a member of the Rajya Sabha until the previous month.

Once our rooms were ready, Mr Yajee sent for the manager and said, 'These Bangladeshi freedom fighters are my guests. So please make sure that their stay here is as comfortable as possible. And another thing, please provide them with anything they ask for.'

We thanked Ganguly'da for arranging such an excellent place for us. After taking a rest, we met Mr Yajee in the lobby again. We showed him the message of Bangabandhu, which we were carrying with us, and the various letters we had received in Agartala, Kolkata and Lucknow. We told him that we wanted to see the Prime Minister. We also wanted to visit various embassies to apply for our visas.

Immediately Mr Yajee telephoned the Prime Minister's secretary. After finishing the telephone call, he told us, 'I have asked the Prime Minister's Secretary to squeeze in a slot for you to meet the Prime Minister as soon as possible.' He also told us that the Prime Minister's secretary would see us first to discuss our meeting.

Accordingly, we met the Prime Minister's secretary, who arranged for us to see the Prime Minister on the following day, 11 May 1972.

When we reached the Prime Minister's Residence, the officials asked us to wait in the lobby. They informed us that the PM was seeing some delegates and would see us soon.

We could see several people standing in a queue on the

lawn. Then we noticed that the Prime Minister was seeing those people in the garden! This scene reminded me of Tagore's famous educational institute, Shantiniketan, in West Bengal. It is a tradition for students at Shantiniketan to receive lessons in the open air. No tables or chairs, and the students sit on the ground! Here the people waiting to see the Prime Minister were on their feet.

She had a garland made of small fresh flowers wrapped around her wrist. We were awestruck when Mrs Gandhi entered the lobby. We were amazed by her extraordinary radiant presence. We felt overwhelmed by the compelling aura around her. She was so distinguishable from others that I could imagine anyone would identify her as a unique person in a big crowd!

Mrs Gandhi greeted us with a warm smile. However, her smiling face and friendly personality could not hide the sign of her confident character and enormous power.

First, we showed her a copy of Bangabandhu's letter, asking us to convey his good wishes to the people of the countries we visited. We then presented her with the decorated flag of Bangladesh and said, 'We acknowledge your support for our cause and for helping us in every possible way.' Finally, we finished our introductory speech by saying, 'Without your support and all the help, it would be a long struggle for us to get our independence.'

Mrs Gandhi was pleased with our gift and accepted it gracefully. She congratulated us for winning the liberation war and appreciated our goodwill mission. Then she led us to a room inside.

FREE PRESS JOURNAL, JUNE 7, 1972 • PAGE THREE

WITH THE PM: The four Bangladesh cyclists presenting Prime Minister Indira Gandhi with their national flag when they called on her in Delhi recently.

Four Dacca students here

By A Staff Reporter

Four students of Dacca University are on a world tour by bicycle "to convey the heartiest message of goodwill and good wishes of the people of Bangladesh to the people of various countries of the world".

After meeting Prime Minister Indira Gandhi in New Delhi and other dignitaries in several States, the four youths, all members of the Mukti Bahini, have now arrived in Bombay. They will shortly be leaving for Cochin from where they intend to take a ship for the Russian port of Odessa.

On this world tour, sponsored by the Bangladesh Foreign Ministry, the Dacca University and the Bangladesh Sports Association, the youths, Jamal Uddin Mohammed Hasan (25), Anwar Uddin Ahmed (20), Mahmud Abdul Quayum (24) and Syed Akhtar Ali (25), will be visiting Russia, Poland, East Germany, West Germany, Czechoslovakia, Greece, Yugoslavia, Rumania, Hungary, Austria, Switzerland, Spain, Italy, France and U.K.

They will be travelling for 1-1½ years on bicycles presented by an Indian cycle manufacturer.

Their proudest possession is their autograph book containing separate one-line messages written by Prime Minister Indira Gandhi for each of them, with her autograph beneath each in both English and Bengali.

The four exhortations by Smt. Gandhi are:

Be courageous and all the rest will follow;

A sense of adventure is war's greatest asset;

Learn to change adversity with opportunity;

With all good wishes.

'Four Dacca students here' is a re-production of a news article published in Free Press Journal, Mumbai, on 7 June 1972, covering our meeting with Indian Prime Minister, Mrs Indira Gandhi.

Once we settled down, she asked us about our route, which countries we would visit next and so on. We explained that, as none of the Middle East countries had recognised Bangladesh as yet, we could not pass through them. Mrs Gandhi appreciated our concern and suggested that we did not have any option but to fly to a European country and resume our journey. We took the opportunity to express our wish that we would prefer to travel to a European country by ship, which would help us to rest. Cycling in India in the scorching heat drained our energy. A journey by ship would allow us to rest long before facing Europe.

'I think it's an excellent idea,' Mrs Gandhi said, and she suggested that we see and discuss arranging our journey to a European country by ship with the shipping minister.

I asked Mrs Gandhi if she would be kind enough to write something in our autograph book. She smiled and said, 'With pleasure,' and took all four autograph books one by one and wrote different wishes for each of us. In my book,

Mrs Gandhi wrote, 'Learn to change adversity into opportunity'.

Mrs Gandhi signed her autograph both in English and Bengali. Immediately I remembered that she once had been a student at Tagore's Shantiniketan.

Looking back at the various events in our journey, we all felt that meeting Mrs Gandhi was one of the highlights of our tour. Most newspapers in India covered the news of our meeting with Prime minster India Gandhi.

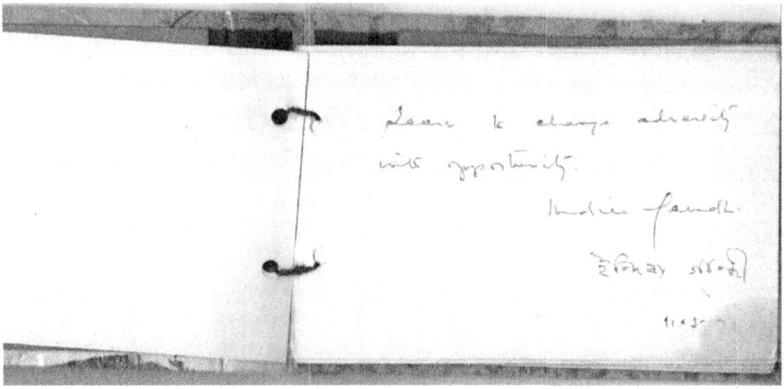

Mrs Indira Gandhi's autograph

We did not have time to relax and explore Delhi until we had secured our visas for the European countries and sorted out our transport to a European country. Mr Yajee contacted the Shipping Minister and arranged for an appointment. He also got Ganguly'da to help us visit the various European embassies.

Ganguly'da gave us the addresses of the embassies of various European countries. He also gave us his car and driver and said, 'Use my car as long as you need to visit all the embassies.' We thanked him for his generous offer.

Suddenly we became busy with lots of tasks at hand. Although our main focus was obtaining visas, we remained engaged with several other unavoidable activities.

We also had an invitation from All India Radio to visit their office for an interview.

One day, when we returned to the hostel in the evening,

the manager gave us an envelope sent to us by a courier. The envelope had the logo of the BBC. We hurriedly opened the letter and were delighted to see the letter was from the BBC Bureau chief, Mr Mark Tully, with an open invitation to drop in at the BBC office as soon as we could manage.

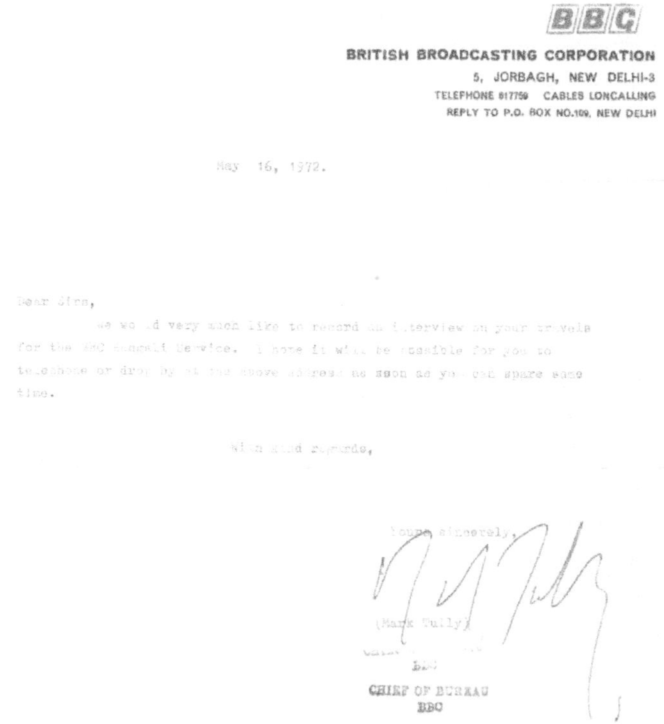

BRITISH BROADCASTING CORPORATION
5, JORBAGH, NEW DELHI-3
TELEPHONE 617759 CABLES LONCALLING
REPLY TO P.O. BOX NO.109, NEW DELHI

May 16, 1972.

Dear Sirs,

We would very much like to record an interview on your travels for the BBC Bengali Service. I hope it will be possible for you to telephone or drop by at the above address as soon as you can spare some time.

With kind regards,

Yours sincerely,

(Mark Tully)

CHIEF OF BUREAU
BBC

Letter from BBC's Mark Tully

In the Indian sub-continent, Mark Tully was a popular name, and there was hardly anyone who did not know of him. Moreover, during the liberation war, the BBC was one of the most reliable radio stations, and most people would tune in to it. So we looked at our diary and decided to meet this famous person, and most importantly, to appear in this world-famous media.

Mr Yajee had arranged for us to see the Shipping Minister. He volunteered to accompany us to the Minister's office. The shipping Minister warmly greeted us and wanted to know how soon we would be able to make ourselves ready to board the ship. We explained that we wished to reach Europe before the winter, and we expected to be in Mumbai early the next month. 'No problem. I will keep you informed of the schedule of ships departing from Mumbai in the next month.'

Suddenly we became swamped with various tasks. We thought appearing in the radio interviews should be our top priority. We attended both radio interviews. We reminded ourselves that the primary purpose of our tour was to convey the good wishes of our Prime Minister and the people of Bangladesh to the people of the world. At that time, television was not widely accessible, and a few people would read the newspapers. However, most people would listen to the radio.

So we attended All India Radio on 16 May 1972. Soon after the All India radio interview, we attended the BBC office where we had the opportunity of meeting the famous person, Mr Mark Tully, head of the BBC.

With BBC's Mark Tully

We were pleased with these two interviews. Then, after obtaining visas for several European countries, including Greece, Yugoslavia, Switzerland, Germany, Belgium and France, we took some time for sightseeing in and around Delhi.

India Gate

One day, we were travelling on the Rajpath when we were struck by the sight of the India Gate, an enormous, imposing edifice. We had heard so much about India Gate, but seeing it in such proximity was awesome.

It has been standard practice for many countries to build a monument, an Edifice, a Minar or some other permanent structure to mark an event or an occasion so that people in future can remember the occasion.

Saheed Minar was built to remember Martyrs Day, on 21 February, in Bangladesh. On 21 February 1952, five people became martyrs during a protest against Pakistan's attempt to abolish our mother tongue and impose a foreign language on us. Therefore we commemorate the language movement day every 21 February and assemble at the Saheed Minar to pay our homage to the language movement martyrs who sowed the seeds for our independence. The date of 21 February has now become International Mother Language Day, and it is celebrated all over the world.

The architectural style of the India Gate is similar to another famous monumental arch, the Arc de Triomphe in Paris. Like the Arc de Triomphe, the India Gate was built as a war memorial to commemorate the British Indian soldiers who fought and lost their lives during the First World War. Originally called the All India War Memorial, the foundation stone of the Gate was laid on 10 February 1921 by the Duke of Connaught. It took ten years to complete the construction. Many important roads spread out from the Gate. It is surrounded by a lush, green garden flanked by clean waters.

During our liberation war in 1971, India had a military confrontation with Pakistan, and in that war, many Indian soldiers lost their lives. Prime Minister Indira Gandhi took the initiative to construct another monument to commemorate the soldiers who lost their lives. This Monument is called 'Amar Jawan Jyoti', the flame of the immortal soldier. It is a cenotaph made of black marble. 'Amar Jawan' is scripted in gold on all four sides of the Monument. On the top, an upside-down rifle stands among the helmets of the unknown soldiers. The base is bound by four urns, one of which holds a continuously burning flame. Mrs Gandhi officially inaugurated the Monument on 26 January 1972. Since 1972, on Republic Day, the President, Prime Minister, Chiefs of the Air, Navy and Army Staff, and assembled dignitaries place a wreath there and pay their respects to the dead.

Red Fort

After seeing the India Gate, we headed towards Old Delhi to visit the famous Red Fort. Emperor Shah Jahan built the Red Fort in 1638. For over two hundred years, it was the main residence of all the Mughal Emperors.

Emperor Shahjahan asked his leading architect, Ahmad Lahauri, to build the Red Fort when Lahauri had already started building the Taj Mahal in Agra. Ahmad Lahauri worked on both projects simultaneously, and both these monuments would become some of the most talked-about structures in the world.

The Red Fort appears as a highly secure and robust structure. It was beyond anybody's imagination that invaders could ever breach it. However, it proved to be so weak and insecure that several invaders invaded on many occasions. The last Mughal Emperor had to escape from the Fort for the safety of his life.

Each time the Red Fort was invaded, the invaders plundered it and looted precious jewels. Iran's Persian Emperor, Nadir shah, carried out the first invasion in 1739. He stole valuable articles, including the precious gems and jewels attached to the famous Peacock Throne. The last invader was the British. After the fall of the Mughal Empire, whatever was left inside the Red Fort was looted by the British. They sold their booty to private collectors and donated some of it to the British Museum, the British Library and the Victoria and Albert Museum. Shah Jahan's jade wine cup and other valuable jewels are all currently located in London. However, after all these lootings and assaults, the Red Fort still looked gorgeous. We wondered how it looked before it lost its original glory.

On 15 August 1947, when India became independent from Britain, Jawaharlal Nehru, the first prime Minister, hoisted the national flag at the Red Fort and delivered a speech. Since then, it has become a tradition for all Indian Prime Ministers to hoist the National flag at the Red Fort on 15 August every year.

Rashtrapati Bhavan

We did not, unfortunately, have the time to see the Rashtrapati Bhavan extensively. However, one has to appreciate this gorgeous palace. By Indian standards, it is a new edifice built at the turn of the 20th century. However, it looked better than many other old edifices because of its unique architecture and the enormity of its size.

Before the capital of British India was moved from Kolkata to Delhi, the Governor used to live in the Government House in Kolkata. Lord Wellesley decreed that India deserved to be governed from a palace, a proper seat of imperial power, rather than a country house. – however grand

– and ordered construction to begin. It took nearly seventeen years for the British architect, Edwin Lutyens, to complete the building work. Lutyens was asked to build the Viceroy's Residence to look like a palace.

In front of the Rastrapati Bhavan

And what a gorgeous palace it is. The Viceroy's House is one of the few architectural features in India which blends Eastern and Western flavours.

After independence, the former Viceroy's house was renamed 'Rashtrapati Bhavan' (the President's Palace). The first Indian President, Rajendra Prasad, became the first occupant. The main building, which includes the president's official residence, reception halls, guest rooms and offices, is part of a structure that contains three hundred and forty rooms. In addition, there are Mughal Gardens, large open spaces, and homes for bodyguards and staff. Built on a site of 320 acres, the Rashtrapati Bhavan is the largest residence of any head of state in the world.

Qutub Minar

Since childhood, we have read about Qutub Minar in our school books. It was the tallest tower in the world and a wonderful minaret. Nowadays, many buildings and towers are much taller than the Qutub Minar. However, the Qutub Minar remains the tallest brick-built tower ever built. It is unlikely that any architect will ever construct a brick-built tower in modern days when other alternatives and better materials are available.

For this reason, the Qutub Minar's record is likely to remain unbroken.

Sometime in 1192, Qutb-ud-din Aibak, who founded the Delhi Sultanate, built the Qutub Minar as a victory tower. However, he only completed the first floor. The construction work continued until 1369 when different sultans commissioned it. Ultimately, it took over four centuries to complete the work.

In front of Qutub Minar

It was a thrilling experience climbing to the top of the Qutub Minar. We had a bird's eye view from there and felt as if we saw the whole of Delhi from there!

After seeing Qutub Minar, as planned, we decided to revisit Uttar Pradesh; we had not yet seen the Taj Mahal. At that time, we were anxious to reach Delhi urgently and, therefore, took a shortcut route from Lucknow. We also knew that Agra would be on the way from Delhi to Mumbai, our final destination in India.

In front of Qutub Minar

We informed Mr Yajee and Ganguly'da that we would be leaving Delhi soon. Ganguli'da told us that one of his friends, Mr Tombi Singh, a Lok Sabha member, had invited us for dinner. Mr Tombi Singh was from Manipur. Manipur is an Indian state in Northeast of India and very close to Bangladesh.

We also discovered that he was a close friend of Mr Yajee, and we were glad to know that Mr Yajee would visit Mr Tombi Singh with us.

On top of Qutub Minar

At the dinner table in Mr Tombi Singh's house, we tasted a range of delicious Manipuri dishes, close to Bangladeshi cuisine.

After a hearty dinner and an interesting after-dinner discussion, which continued until late, it was time to say goodbye to Mr Tombi Singh and Ganguli'da. We thanked Mr Singh for the invite and regretted that we had not had the opportunity of meeting him earlier. The next day was the most challenging moment for us as we said goodbye to our father figure, Mr Yajee. We became emotional and were in tears. Mr Yajee blessed us with good wishes for our journey. We thought of thanking him elaborately but felt we could not express our feelings appropriately in words. Finally, however, we had to say something so that he knew how grateful we were to him. While Akhtar, Babul and Khokan expressed their gratitude with misty eyes, I felt the need to say something to express my true feeling for him. So I said, 'We must have done some very good deeds in the past to have met you'. We told him that his blessing would protect us from all adversity we might face in the future.

TWELVE

Agra

Leaving Delhi, we headed towards Agra. We focused our minds on one thought; that soon we would see the Taj Mahal.

Since we were children, we have heard so much about this beautiful Monument. Not only that it was one of the most beautiful buildings in the world, but it was about an emperor's unprecedented love for his wife. We had always dreamt of seeing this wonder.

We temporarily held back on our dream of seeing the Taj Mahal and decided to visit Emperor Akbar's tomb in Sikandra first, which was on the way.

Akbar's Tomb

Before Emperor Akbar the Great died, he planned his tomb and selected Sikandra as his chosen site. After his death, Emperor Jahangir fulfilled his father's wish and built Akbar's tomb. This tomb is one of the most outstanding Mughal architectural masterpieces. It occupies one hundred and nineteen acres of grounds in Sikandra.

Akbar was a Muslim, but he was very secular-minded. His tomb reflected this aspect of his character and blended both Hindu and Muslim architecture. It may be the only tomb of the Mughal emperors where one can find the Hindu Swastika engraved on the walls to represent the Emperor's broad and enriched mind. The Monument is built of a deep red sandstone, and its features are picked out in white marble. The mural designs are geometric, floral and calligraphic. A black slate adorns the tomb. Though he was a Muslim, Akbar married a Hindu princess to unify the Muslims and Hindus. He also used to invite theologians from all religions to take part in theological discussions. He unified the vast Mughal state by adopting conciliatory policies and removing discrimination based on faith. He is known as 'Akbar the Great' for enlarging the Mughal Empire, but also for ruling his subjects successfully and peacefully. No other Mughal emperor came close to comparing with Akbar.

Taj Mahal

After an enjoyable tour of Akbar's tomb, we headed towards Agra, just a few kilometres from Sikandra. We were lucky to find a B&B very close to the Taj Mahal. Leaving our bikes in the hotel, we hurriedly went out again. We wanted to see the Taj Mahal at once!

When we had our first glimpse of the Monument through the enormous entrance gate, we felt it had been worth waiting for all these years to view this wonder with our own eyes. Once we passed the Gate, we were on one of the two parallel pathways. There were two rows of beautiful gardens with manicured plants, and a wide strip of water with fountains between the pathways. The vivid image was breathtaking. The Taj Mahal exceeded our expectations!

At Taj Mahal

Taj Mahal

At Taj Mahal

While looking at the Monument, I remember saying, 'No wonder this monument is one of the Seven Wonders of the World.' The white marble building stunned me and made me realise that it was not the same as seeing a photograph. It was something entirely different looking at it through my own eyes. Standing there, I felt that the rest of the world was insignificant.

The Taj Mahal was built following the description of heaven given in the Holy Qur'an; like a garden with fountains surrounding it.

The flowing water between the pathways is essential for a paradise garden. Many experts claim that the Taj Mahal garden is intended to resemble the description of 'The Kausar Fountain' mentioned in the holy Qur'an. We walked around the Monument, saw it from different angles and went inside. The whole place was buzzing with the spectators' exclamations and excited expressions; but once we were inside, we felt the heavy silence and a sombre atmosphere, particularly at the sites of the two tombs: that of Emperor Shah Jahan and, of course, his wife, and the object of his great love, Mumtaz Mahal. Later we learned that those tombs were cenotaphs and that their actual graves were nearby, underground.

Taj Mahal

We had heard that the view of the Taj Mahal from the Agra fort was better than seeing it from proximity. We also learnt that we could go to the room in the Agra Fort, across the Jumna River, where Shah Jahan gazed out at the Taj Mahal during his final years. So we decided to come back to see the Taj Mahal again, but to see it from Agra Fort first.

There have been comments by many people that the Taj Mahal had nothing to do with Shajahan's eternal love for his wife but that it was an arrogant demonstration of his power. However, once we study the history in detail, we find that Prince Khurram (later given the title of 'Shah Jahan') and his childhood friend, Anjumand (later given the title 'Mumtaj Mahal' after her marriage), had been engaged for five years. They had to wait five years for the court astrologers to select a suitable wedding date to ensure a happy marriage. And who can disagree about how happy this marriage was? Shajahan and Mumtaz were so close to each other that Mumtaz Mahal would be with Shaj Jahan even when he was on the battlefield.

Mumtaz was heavily pregnant with her 14th child when Shajahan was engaged in a war in south India. Even in that condition, she accompanied Shajahan to the battlefield. Unfortunately, she died during childbirth, far away from the palace. After Mumtaz Mahal died, the Emperor was empty; he kept himself in seclusion for a whole year. He was finally lured out of his reclusive existence by his eldest daughter, Jahanara Begum. He then determined to build the most magnificent tomb the world had ever known to celebrate his love for the deceased empress. It took twenty years for

20,000 artisans engaged from far-off Baghdad and Bukhara to construct the Taj Mahal. Rumour has it that Shahjahan himself planned, designed and oversaw the construction of the world's most famous and beautiful mausoleum.

When his son Aurangzeb took the throne, he imprisoned Shahjahan at the Agra Fort near the Taj Mahal. The former Emperor gazed at the Taj Mahal from his balcony in the Jasmine Tower every day for the last eight years.

Agra Fort

Agra was the main residence of the Mughal emperors until the capital was moved to Delhi in 1638. When we visited Agra, we learned that it is the largest and one of the oldest fortresses in India. However, no one knows who built this Fort and exactly when. Though Agra's history is primarily associated with the Mughal Empire, the fortress was established much earlier. It has links with the Mahabharata in 3 BC. Different rulers have occupied it at different times in history. Each ruler renovated and enlarged the building according to their power, ability and need. It is believed that the earliest occupier was Rajput King Raja Badal Singh, who named Fort, Badalgarh. After that, the name was changed to the Red Fort and then again to Agra Fort.

Emperor Akbar carried out extensive renovation work. First, he built a long fortress wall. After that, successive Mughal emperors built additional palaces inside the Fort.

Emperor Humayun found enormous treasures hidden there, including the famous hand-cut diamond that Humayun called Kohinoor.

We cut short our tour as we were eager to view the Taj Mahal from the Jasmine Tower. While we were there, we overheard the conversation of other tourists that on the full moon, the view of the Taj Mahal from the Jasmine Tower was genuinely dreamy. We also learned about the mystery of the Taj Mahal changing its colour at different times of the day. It looks pearly grey or sometimes pale pink at sunrise but changes to dazzling white by noon. It changes its colour to orange in the sunset. But it looks dreamy in the evenings and appears as a translucent blue. We thought of visiting at different times of the day to experience the varying appearances of this mysterious Monument.

Our second visit was in the early evening. We were surprised to see how it changed its appearance during sunset. Slowly the sunlight made it glow reddish with a tinge of gold. Then when it was getting darker, we saw it change again. The golden dress slowly transformed into pale blue. Unfortunately, in the absence of full strong moonlight, the Monument mainly remained the same. Therefore, we had to stretch our imaginations about how the strong moonlight would make the Taj Mahal the most beautiful object.

The Taj Mahal is one of the supreme wonders of Mughal architecture. We felt we had just made a lifelong dream come true. And it was as magical as I had hoped. Emperor Shahjahan is considered the ultimate lover because he immortalised his legendary love for his wife, creating the Taj Mahal. We heard many interesting stories surrounding this world-famous Monument. According to a popular legend, Shah Jahan cut off the hands of the builders and gouged out their eyes so that no one could imitate the Taj Mahal's beauty. He ensured that the Taj Mahal remains an exquisite masterpiece without an equal.

Initially, inside the Taj Mahal, there was only one cenotaph honouring Mumtaz Mahal, and Shah Jahan wished to have his Monument opposite the Taj Mahal in black marble. However, after his death, his plan was abandoned. Instead, an extra cenotaph was placed beside Mumtaz Mahal.

Another exciting story is that before Shah Jahan selected the artisans, he took them to the seashore and asked them to throw valuables into the water. He rejected any who hesitated or refused to do so. He selected only those workers who would not hesitate to spend more than was necessary to achieve his architectural dream.

After seeing the Taj Mahal on two to three occasions, we decided to pop in to see another monument close to the Agra Fort. It's called the Itmad-ud-Daulah's Tomb. This tomb is one of the most impressive architectural wonders of the city of Agra. It is also known as the 'Baby Taj Mahal', as it is widely believed that this tomb inspired the creation of the Taj Mahal.

THIRTEEN

Ajmer Sharif *Dargah* (Shrine)

After seeing various outstanding monuments in Agra, we were on our way to Mumbai, crossing Rajasthan, the largest state in India. Besides being the largest, Rajasthan has a prestigious background. The name Rajasthan means the home of the Rajas.

Although there are many great sights in Rajasthan, we resisted the temptation to stop at Jaipur, the capital of Rajasthan or visit other big cities like Udaipur or Jodhpur. This was not just to avoid the hot desert environment but, most importantly, because of our eagerness to reach Mumbai as soon as possible to sort out our onward journey to Europe. Moreover, we didn't want to miss our boat. Finally, however, we decided to visit Ajmer Sharif on the way to Mumbai.

Ajmer Sharif

Khwaja Moinuddin Chisti was a twelfth-century Iranian Sufi teacher and philosopher; in 1192, he arrived in India to preach Islam. He was, it is said, a direct descendant of Prophet Mohammad. Chisti chose to live in Ajmer, a place in Rajasthan already recognised as holy by the Hindu and Sikh religions. Chisti lived in Ajmer until he died in March 1236. During his life in Ajmer, he became a well-known preacher and spiritual leader. After his death, he was widely regarded as a saint, and his tomb soon became one of the most famous shrines in India.

Chisti enjoyed royal patronage, since the very first Sultan, all the rulers in Delhi were patrons of the Dargah. After the demise of the Delhi Sultanate, the Mughal Dynasty became the power in Delhi. Emperor Akbar was the first Mughal Emperor to visit the Dargah, and he was very impressed by Dargah's popularity. Akbar was about to engage in a complex war. He pledged that if he were victorious in the forthcoming battle, he would go on a pilgrimage to the Dargah.

He kept his word and visited the Dargah on foot, like a traditional pilgrim. Akbar did not have a son and decided to meet Selim Chisti, the successor of Moinuddin Chisti, to ask for his blessing. Subsequently, Emperor Akbar had three sons. His first son, Selim, later became Emperor Jahangir. From that moment on, Akbar was a frequent visitor to the Dargah. Every time Emperor Akbar went there, he made generous donations to the Dargah and the people running the Dargah. At one point, he reconstructed the Dargah and, as time went by, became deeply involved with its development. He arranged for a permanent endowment for the Dargah's maintenance and underwrote the running costs of the *Langar Khana* (free food). Over time, the tomb became popularly known as the 'Ajmer Sharif' and was the most famous religious shrine for Muslims and other religious groups.

Emperor Akbar commissioned a colossal chandelier, the

Sahn Chirag. In addition, the Golden temple donated a large silver chandelier.

As time passed, the number of pilgrims grew. The Dargah complex expanded accordingly. There are quite a few entrance gates, each built at different times by different donors. Mir Osman Ali Khan, the seventh Nizam of Hyderabad, commissioned the main entrance of the Dargah. Mughal emperor Shahjahan had built the older Gate, known as Shahjahani Gate. The expansion of the Dargah continued for centuries, and the Dargah enjoyed royal patronage until the Mughal dynasty disintegrated. However, in the absence of the Sultans, Emperors, Kings/Queens and other royal personalities have continued the flow of donations to the Dargah. As a result, the popularity of the Dargah has never diminished. And the number of pilgrims has continued to increase. It is thought that Queen Mary of Teck (wife of King George V) may have made the last royal donation to the Dargah and provided additional water tanks for the pilgrims in 1911. Nowadays, contributions come mainly from pilgrims from all over the world. The pilgrims make cash donations, which help run the Dargah. The pilgrims bring over seven tonnes of rose petals daily. The other typical donation is 'Chadors' (multipurpose garments), which are treated as sacred sheets. Recently the Indian Prime Minister, Narendra Modi, gave Ajmir Dargah a golden 'Chador'.

The regular daily activities in the Dargah start at dawn and last until the evening throughout the year. The recital of daily prayers, lighting rituals, and the singing of Qawaali (songs praising the Prophet) are exciting events in the

Dargah. The Dargah also provides free food to the approximately 20,000 pilgrims who visit the site daily. This food is the same as Khawja Chisti consumed. When Emperor Akbar visited the Dargah, he waited in a queue and took the *Langar* food like any other ordinary pilgrim.

There is no restriction on women entering the Dargah.

On the anniversary of Moinuddin Chisti's death, there are six days of activities and rituals when pilgrims from all over the world pour into Ajmer. The number of pilgrims equals the total population of Ajmer! It becomes necessary to arrange special train and bus services during that time.

While visiting Hindu and Buddhist temples in Banaras, we observed that the pilgrims were from different religious backgrounds. Ajmer Sharif was no exception. We learned with interest about the active involvement of non-Muslims with the Dargah. For example, it is traditional for a Hindu Brahmin family to supply incense, sandalwood paste, and attar (a fragrant essential oil) to the Dargah; this has its roots in the time of Chisti. Rose petals for the Dargah come from Pushker, a holy Hindu and Sikh site about nine miles from the Dargah.

Many pilgrims visit a shrine/holy place when they face difficulties and wish to get the saint's blessings to overcome their hardships. Other pilgrims visit a holy place because, in the past, they pledged to visit a shrine when they successfully achieved their goals. Being in Banaras and Ajmer Sharif, I felt that there must be a third group who did not visit a shrine with specific demands or expectations or because they had pledged to visit a shrine. Some pilgrims visit a holy place in order to purify their souls or simply feel happy being in a peaceful place. I wondered which group we belonged to. We did not visit Ajmer Sharif with any specific expectations. We did not strictly fall under the third group either. However, when we were leaving the Dargah, I wondered whether we subconsciously hoped that visiting holy places would help our goodwill mission be trouble-free and successful.

FOURTEEN

On the Way to Mumbai

Having seen Ajmer Sharif, we headed towards Mumbai, our last destination in India.

We had been busy in Delhi obtaining visas for European countries; now, we expected to finalise our onward journey from India. However, we did not know when our ship would sail from Mumbai. For this reason, we wanted to reach Mumbai as soon as possible and decided not to visit many tourist spots on the way. However, there are one or two events that remain in our minds.

Since leaving Agra, we had consumed the most boring food, day after day. The typical lunch and dinner had been chapatti or oven-baked, thick roti with dhal and yoghurt. We were dying to taste familiar food. One day we stopped by a roadside restaurant that looked quite impressive.

Realising that we were Bengali, the manager raised our expectations and said, 'If you are not in a hurry, we could cook rice for you. Rice is our staple food, and the thought that we would get rice made our mouths water immediately. We were starving, but the expectation of having rice made us determined to wait. We thought it would take just half an hour or a little longer, but it would be worth waiting. After waiting nearly an hour, we enquired about the delay.

The manager said the rice was being cooked and told us it wouldn't be long. Seeing no one in the kitchen, we asked ourselves who was cooking the rice. The manager took us out and showed us some cooked rice spread on a bench under the sun to dry! We realised that the rice had become too soggy, and the cook had tried to make it presentable. If we had any idea that the cook didn't know how to cook rice, we would have volunteered to cook this simplest of all dishes ourselves!

To our pleasant surprise, however, there was a hot vegetable curry with dhal. Because we were so hungry that we could eat anything, soggy rice and hot vegetable tasted most delicious. We gobbled down the food in no time and did not care if we made complete pigs of ourselves!

Since we had left Banaras, we tried to avoid riding in the hot afternoon. This was thanks to the advice from Colonel Singh. 'Don't ride bikes in the sun. Always be on the road early in the morning and stop when the temperature increases.' We followed his advice, always tried to start early morning, and then took a long break to pass the hot afternoon whenever possible. But unfortunately, the temperature often started rising long before eleven o'clock.

One day, after riding for a couple of hours in the early morning, we stopped when we reached a small town. According to our assessment, we were not very far from Mumbai. We wishfully thought this might be the outskirts of Mumbai. We were pleased to learn that the place we had stopped at was called Thane, and it was only thirty kilometres from Mumbai.

We decided to rest for a short while and looked for a suitable place. While we were doing this, we drew the attention of a gentleman who realised we were tourists from Bangladesh. He approached us and introduced himself as Mr Das. The name indicated that he was Bengali. He said, 'My parents came to India from Bengal (East Pakistan and now Bangladesh) during the partition in 1947.' Mr Das was keen to tell us about his background. He told us that his parents and relatives were settled in Kolkata. However, He had left Kolkata when he found his present job as the plant manager of a textile factory in Thane. Mr Das cordially invited us to his home, where we could rest for a while.

While we were munching delicious snacks, Mr Das contacted his boss and explained about us. His boss became very interested in meeting us. But unfortunately, he was not working that day. He asked Mr Das to take us to the company's guest house and make arrangements for us to stay there.

We explained to Mr Das that we needed to reach Mumbai urgently and had no time to relax. But he insisted that we see the company's guest house. We were stunned to see the most luxurious guest house, complete with a swimming pool. We had never seen such a posh place before. Mr Das explained that their company produced garments mainly for export to various countries. The guest house entertained the company's potential customers who visited them from abroad. He informed us that Raymond Ltd. is the largest integrated manufacturer of fabric in the world. While we were still looking at the beautiful swimming pool, he told us that his boss had asked him to run the water in the pool so we could relax. We thanked him and explained that we had to be in Mumbai before the offices closed. He then tried to persuade us to have a tour of the enormous factory. We promised him we would try to visit the factory and meet his boss later if time permitted.

It was tempting to accept the invitation, but we were concerned about knowing the date when the ship would sail.

FIFTEEN

Mumbai

Reaching Mumbai, we were astounded to see skyscrapers for the first time. We had been to a few cities, but Mumbai looked quite different. A touch of European flavour was evident. We didn't have time to appreciate the cosmopolitan city. We rushed to the Tube Investment of India office. They had branches in most cities throughout India. They had kindly agreed to act as our care-of-address. After the small talk, we collected letters from relatives and friends. We continued our discussion about the tour so far. Tube Investment was happy when we gave them the good news that there had been no issues with the cycles, and we were delighted with the most reliable bikes we could have. We promised to keep them informed of our tour from time to time.

Leaving the Tube Investment office, we headed towards the shipping corporation office to find out the date of our departure from India.

The officials cordially received us at the Shipping Corporation. The manager, Mr S. R. Prasad, greeted us with a smile and said, 'I am so relieved that you are finally here. I was expecting your arrival any day.' While we were talking, I took out Mr Bheemappa's letter. Mr Prasad glanced at the letter and told us that he had already received the letter and, subsequently, received a few telephone calls from Mr Bheemappa about us.

Seeing Mr Prasad so cheerful, I expected the manager to tell us that we had not missed the boat and that the ship was sailing very soon. However, I was wrong. He did not mention anything on this subject. The small talk continued while he led us to his office. Once we settled down, cold drinks arrived, but there was no sign of him giving us the news that we had been eagerly waiting to hear. Instead, he excused himself for a second and sent for one of his colleagues. He broke the news that no ship was scheduled to sail from Mumbai to Europe at that time. However, he had been authorised to arrange our flight to Athens. We did not expect to hear this news.

Naturally, we had mixed feelings. On the one hand, we would reach Athens quickly and have the whole summer in Europe before the winter arrived. But on the other hand, we needed a long rest before covering Europe. We asked whether we had missed a boat and, if so, when would be the next boat sailing to Athens. We explained our reasons. The manager thought for a second and then phoned a colleague. He said we could, catch a vessel sailing for Athens – but not from Mumbai. He told us that the next ship, in fact, one of the giant cargo ships of India, would be sailing from Cochin on 22 June 1972. We slumped in our chairs and said it would be impossible to reach Cochin in such a short time. The manager continued, 'We can arrange for you to fly to Cochin so that you will not need to bike all the way.' We looked at each other, readily agreed to this proposal and thanked him profoundly. In the meantime, a gentleman entered the room and introduced himself as Mr Pachu Gopal. He was a talkative person. 'I am so pleased to meet you. I am proud of the freedom fighters...'

Mr Prasad intervened and told us, 'Mr Gopal has kindly agreed to make arrangements for you to stay at his place.' As tourists, we were used to staying anywhere; but we were concerned that it would be too much for Mr Gopal to put us up for nearly two weeks. At that point, Mr Gopal started speaking Bengali to inform us about his ethnicity. He said he was born in Barisal, a Southern District of Bangladesh. It would be a pleasure to have us as his guests. We were delighted to have a Bengali host and immediately followed the Bengali culture of addressing him by 'Gopal'da', meaning brother Gopal.

After our discussion with the Shipping Corporation, we went to Gopal'da's house, not far from the city centre. Besides his wife, a little girl and his mother, no one else lived in his big house. Staying with a Bengali family, we felt very fortunate. However, after a day or two, we realised that Gopalda's wife was not Bengali and was from Bangalore. However, she fooled us with her fluency in Bengali and being a keen admirer of Tagore's songs.

Gopal'da was an engineer. Before joining the Shipping Corporation, he was involved with installing the lighting system of the Queen's Necklace. Seeing our puzzled look, he explained that the 'C' shaped Marine Drive lighting is known as 'the *Queen's Necklace'*. These street lights resemble a string of pearls in a necklace. He told us he would take us to see the Queen's Necklace after dinner.

When we were close to Marine Drive, we felt the difference in the air and the temperature. It was cooler, and the air quality seemed much better than in the city. As soon as Gopal'da entered the Marine Drive, we couldn't help but utter the word, 'Wow'. He said he would drive from one end to the other of the nearly three-mile stretch and would stop somewhere in the middle so we could join hundreds of people who were enjoying the evening in the most pleasant atmosphere. Marine Drive was a superb promenade. Most people were having a stroll, but some were sitting and absorbing the beauty of the sea and, of course, the Queen's Necklace. The lighting on Marine Drive looked beautiful. We told Gopal'da, 'You must be a very proud man to have been involved in creating this breathtaking scene!' Although we had never been to a promenade in Europe, we could imagine what it would feel like to stroll on a European promenade. The Queen's Necklace on Marine Drive gave us European vibes in India.

While driving back, Gopal'da informed us that most people in Mumbai were aware of our presence in the city from various newspapers. He specifically told us that the Indo-Bangla Friendship Society in Mumbai was eager to meet us.

As we had some time on our hands, we decided to pay a return visit to Thane to meet Mr Das and his boss. We travelled there by train. Mr Das was delighted to see us and contacted his boss to give him the news. When the CEO arrived and extended his hand to shake ours, we were taken aback at his modest appearance. Unlike his other white-collar workers, he did not wear a tie or a shirt. He was in his T-shirt and wore slippers instead of polished shoes; he said it was too hot to wear shoes. I still remember feeling shocked seeing the NASA chief wearing a T-shirt at a press conference after a successful launch of a space rocket. He didn't care that the whole world would see him in such a simple dress. Seeing the CEO of Raymond Woollen Mills at Thane, I remembered a famous proverb in Bengali. The proverb says that known Brahmins do not need to wear the ***poite*** (a sacred white thread that Brahmins are allowed to wear as a symbol of belonging to the upper caste in Hinduism).

The CEO was also very casual about his dealings with others. He showed us the impressive factory and explained that Raymond Woollen Mills was one of the biggest garment industries in the world. Many years later, I realised that the CEO must have studied in the west and adopted a western attitude.

The CEO insisted that we choose some products as his gifts. Because we were travelling light, we could not afford to be greedy in accepting his offer. However, we agreed to choose a pair of trousers and a T-Shirt each, which helped us maintain our uniform.

After we returned to Mumbai, Gopal'da took us to one of his friend's houses in the evening. He told us that his friend, Mr Banerjee, was one of the lucky people to have an apartment in Mumbai's poshest residential area, on Malabar Hill. In response to our questions, he said, 'No. He is not a businessman. However, he is one of the senior engineers employed by Tata. So you can say that he is one of the few outstanding professionals, rich enough to have an apartment on Malabar Hill.'

Mr and Mrs Banerjee were delighted to have us as their guests. The typical Bengali culture of gossiping started in no time. We found Banerjee'da a humorous person. He kept us amused with witty jokes. Often he sang a parody or two, giving us the impression that he could have been a professional singer.

He then told us a story about something that had happened in Mumbai recently. One evening he went to a Tagore concert in Mumbai where a Sikh artist translated one of the popular Tagore songs, 'Tumi Kemon Kore Gaan Koro Hey Guni'. The proper translation of the lyrics in English goes as follows:

> 'How well you sing, o accomplished artist!
> Stunned, I merely listen.
> The light of your melodies spreads across the world;
> The breeze of your notes flits through the sky,
> Splintered, the stones speed anxiously
> Flowing away in the stream of melodies.
> I feel like singing in the same style,
> But cannot capture the notes.
> What I want to say, I cannot.
> Defeated, my soul cries,
> Weaving a web of notes all around.
> What snares you have lured me into!'

But the singer's poor translation of this song in Hindi distorted the meaning and feeling of the beautiful song altogether. He sang, 'Tu Keisa karke Gaan korta Hey Kobi, mei burbak hoker sonta (How do you sing my poet. I keep listening like a mindless foolish. The cool breezes are coming through the cracked stones ... mei burbak hoker sunta...') A Tagore lover in the audience could not listen any longer. He stood up in disgust and walked out of the concert, shouting, 'You sing like a stupid fool.'

Through Gopal'da, we met the president of the Indo-Bangla Friendship Society, Mr Navin T Khandwalla. The first thing Mr Khandwalla enquired about was how his organisation could help us. He also informed us that the Society's members would be interested in meeting us and he was going to hold a reception for us soon.

At our next meeting, Mr Khadwalla gave us copies of some of the letters he had already despatched to various people. I realised that it was not an empty promise to help us; that he had already taken prompt and practical actions. I also realised that he was involved with many social organisations in Mumbai and his associates belonged to the 'Who's Who of Mumbai. In other words, he was the most influential person among the Mumbai socialites; the rich, cultured and influential people of Mumbai. I noticed him appearing as either the chairperson or the treasurer of various organisations from different letterheads. I was highly impressed seeing the way he got things done.

Mr Khandwalla was not only the chairperson of with Indo Bangla Friendship Society and the chairperson of the Indo-Bangladesh Association but also another organisation, 'Bombay Sairuni of Calcutta University Bangladesh Sahayak SAruni'. Moreover, he seemed involved with various other organisations, like the 'SAIRAM', The Society for Aid, Relief, Rehabilitation & Assistance.

On one occasion, Mr Khandwalla learned from a telegram sent to us by the Bangladesh Foreign Office that it was impossible to get a visa for the USSR on short notice. He immediately wrote a letter to Mr Nikolai V. Aksenov, the Consulate General of the USSR in Mumbai, asking him to issue us with visas for the USSR. However, we asked him not to pursue this as we preferred to go to Athens from Cochin by sea.

Mr Khandwalla was persuasive in his communication with the members. In one letter, he informed the members of the Bombay SAruni of Calcutta University Bangladesh Sahayak SAruni that he was trying to get help for us from his friends and therefore needed the members' permission to spend money on some essentials. He finished his letter by saying that if he did not hear any objection, he would take it that the members agreed to pay the amount from the SAruni's fund. When he learned that we wished to appear on All India Radio, Mumbai, he immediately telephoned the radio station director and arranged for the radio to interview us.

One day, we received an invitation to a party from Dilip Kumar, who is considered one of the all-time greatest actors in the history of Indian Cinema. Dilip Kumar is also known as the first superstar of Bollywood movies. We were excited about this invitation, hoping to meet all the Bollywood stars at the party. However, we quickly realised that the time and date of the party clashed with our radio interview. All my teammates wanted to attend the party at Dilip Kumar's house and cancel the radio interview. It was tempting. However, I explained to my friends that Mr Khandwalla had made a personal request to the radio station director for this interview. It would look bad if we did not attend the interview. Also, we needed to do the radio interview so we could convey our good wishes to millions of people. Fortunately, all my three friends reluctantly agreed, so we attended the radio interview instead of the party. It was just unfortunate that the invitation clashed with another significant engagement.

Gopal'da took us to Banerjee'da's house most evenings

for our gossiping sessions. One evening, Mrs Banerjee informed us that she would introduce us to one of her friends, Mrs Saraladevi Chowguley, who was keen to meet us. Gopal'da immediately commented, 'Mrs Chowguley is one of the richest persons in India. She is the wife of a shipping magnate and involved with several voluntary organisations.'

And so a person we had not even met yet would later become our third mentor in India. Our first mentor was the Bangladesh Diplomat, Anwarul Karim Chowdhury, in Kolkata. The second one was veteran politician Mr Sheelbhadra Yajee in New Delhi.

From our first meeting with Mrs Chowguley, we felt her affection for us, like she was one of our favourite aunties. She was always concerned about helping us. Her love for us was sincere and genuine. But, first, she was worried that we did not have proper accommodation. We said that we were pretty happy staying with Gopal'da. However, she looked for suitable alternative accommodation for us. Shortly afterwards, she arranged for us to move into a decent apartment in the heart of the city. She also allowed us to use one of her cars, with a driver, who would pick us up from our apartment and drop us back in the evening.

In those days, there were no foreign cars on the streets of India. One could only see the Indian-made 'Ambassador' cars. India produced everything it needed and did not rely on foreign commodities. Foreign commodities were banned or highly taxed to encourage people to consume national products. However, because Mrs Chowguley was super-rich, she owned foreign cars. When the chauffeur came to pick us up or drop us back, neighbours would approach the car to see it in detail. They must have wondered: who were those four young men who were lucky enough to ride a foreign car?

Mrs Chowguley acted as our guardian. She advised us about many things, including how to take care of ourselves when touring Europe.

Mr Khandwalla and Mrs Chowguley informed us that they had invited their members to a reception to meet us.

INDO BANGLADESH ASSOCIATION,

Keshav Nivas,
20, Nepeansea Road,
Bombay. 36.

Tel. 366409
351461

THE INDO BANGLADESH ASSOCIATION
request
the pleasure of your comapny at a get-together
to meet
SHRI JAMAL UDDIN MD HASAN
SHRI ANWAR UDDIN AHMED
SHRI MAHMUD ABDUL QUAYUM
SHRI SYED AKHTAR ALI

students of Dacca University and members of the Mukti Bahini (Freedom Fighters) who are on a World Tour on bicycle on a Goodwill Mission. They carry with them the message of their Prime Minister, Sheikh Mujibur Rehman and the blessings of our our Prime Minister, Smt. Indira Gandhi.

at the Gita Mandir, Bharatiya Vidya Bhavan,
Chowpatty, Bombay.7

at 4.30 p.m. on SATURDAY the 10th June, 1972.

Smt. Mehboob Nasrullah, Sheriff of Bombay has kindly agreed to preside over the function.

Invitation to members of the Indo-Bangladesh Association to attend a reception

We were impressed by Mr Khandwalla and Mrs Chowguley's efficiency in organising a successful reception at such short notice.

We found the hall full of enthusiasts. The people on the panel and in the packed house audience it was apparent that these people were distinguished and influential people in Mumbai. All the speakers from the panel praised us for our courage and determination to win the liberation war. They also praised us for undertaking the goodwill mission.

Babul and I spoke at the reception and thanked Indo Bangladesh Association for giving us an impressive reception. We also thanked India for supporting and helping us for our independence. We particularly thanked the Indian people from all walks of life for their generous help and for supporting our struggle.

With some of the Indo Bangladesh Associations members

Mrs Chowguley speaking at the reception

Babul and I spoke at the reception

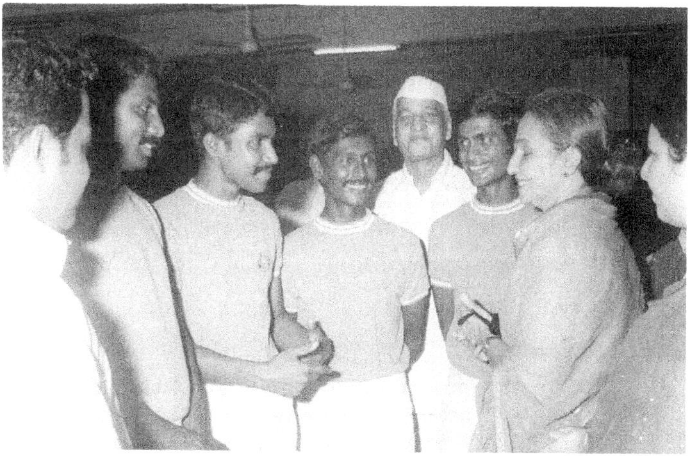

After the formal reception, we had a lively discussion with Mrs Chowguley and other members of the Indo Bangladesh Association.

Babul and I spoke at the reception and acknowledged India's role in looking after the Bangladeshi refugees and helping us win the liberation war by publicising the barbaric genocide by the brutal Pakistan army. We also thanked the people of India for welcoming us and helping us in all possible ways.

One day Mrs Chowguley informed us that her daughter's school wanted to give us a reception. The school was called Villa Theresa Girls High School. It was a Roman Catholic English medium institution in Mumbai. The happy students in the auditorium took me back to my school days when we always loved attending such activities; instead of boring classes.

The teachers, parents and students packed the assembly hall at the reception. First, the Headmistress gave brief background information about the school's role during our liberation war. Then she informed us that the students took an active part in collecting clothes and other articles for the Bangladeshi refugees inside India. They also raised funds to support our liberation war.

Some student representatives spoke at the reception. They thanked us for visiting their school. Then they told us how happy and proud they were to meet us, the courageous freedom fighters who defeated a strong armed force in the world. They were delighted that we had liberated our country. Finally, a very young girl appeared on the stage. The little girl looked at us and, with an innocent smile, said, 'We thank you for visiting us.' Then she gave us an envelope, saying, 'We have made a small collection for you. This is a token of our support for your journey ahead.' This reception made us very emotional as the description of the events they referred to touched us deeply. The children's generous gift significantly moved us.

I looked at Babul, Akhtar and Khokan and was not surprised to see their misty eyes. I stood up to speak. Firstly I thanked the little girl who had handed over the envelope to me. I have never been a good orator, but being in that situation, I tried to give an emotional speech which was something like this:

Reverend sisters and dear friends,

It is too difficult to express our deep sense of gratitude for your good wishes and generous gift. Listening to your help and support for our liberation war reminded us of the life and death situation during our great liberation struggle. We fondly remember your sacrifices as students of this school and other institutions in India, spontaneously collecting essential articles and funds for the Bangladeshi refugees. Your boundless love and affection were the most significant help in our struggle.

Our objectives of travelling the world on bicycles carrying the message of love and goodwill to all are challenging. However, your good wishes will undoubtedly provide us with a source of inspiration. We hope to return to your school one day to tell you about our achievements, failures and glory. We will leave Mumbai on 19 June, and till we return, Good Bye.

Mrs Chowguley converted the Indian Rupees the school raised to dollars as we were about to leave India. After the reception, Mrs Chowguley took us to her house for dinner.

The more we learnt about Mrs Chowguley, the more we liked her. For a super-rich person, she was extremely modest. She always had a smile on her face. Her involvement with social work was very praiseworthy.

Like Mr Yajee, she also teased us from time to time, a sign of a close relationship. At the dining table, she jokingly advised us, 'You are going to Europe. You must be careful of not to fall for White Elephants!'

We then argued with her whether Bangalore (Where Mrs Chowguley came from) or Bangladesh produced better quality mangoes. No one won the argument in the end. She was one of two people from India who contacted us to know how we were doing in Europe and advised us to keep our focus on our aim.

Before we left Mumbai for Cochin, Mr Khandwalla and Mrs Chowguley gave us an envelope marked 'Bon Voyage' addressed to 'The Four World Tourists on cycles from Bangladesh. With compliments' from The Society for Aid, Relief, Rehabilitation & Assistance, Chief Patron: Nawab Ali Yavar Jung, The Governor of Maharashtra. We profoundly thanked everybody in Mumbai who helped us during our stay there.

SIXTEEN

Cochin

Before we left Mumbai on 19 June 1972, the Shipping Corporation of India gave us four air tickets to Cochin, details of our hotel near the port, and documents regarding the bookings of our cabins on the Bishva Prabha. The ship was bound for Odesa through the black sea. On the way, we would get off at the Piraeus seaport in Athens.

As we boarded the plane from Mumbai for Cochin, we cast our minds back to the experiences we had enjoyed in India. We concluded that India was a miniature world of diverse cultures, languages and climate conditions. If someone travelled the whole of India, they would have the experience of travelling the whole world. We felt pleased about our successful tour of India and very relaxed. We were looking forward to the prospect of being able to recharge our run-down batteries during our month-long journey by ship.

After landing at Cochin airport, we headed towards Hotel Casino, approximately 25 miles away. While riding in Cochin, we were amazed by the greenery everywhere. Until then, we believed that no other country was greener than Bangladesh. But Cochin's greenness dented our pride and gave us a new definition of the word 'green'!

It was our first experience staying in a five-star hotel.

For the last few months, we have experienced extremely hot temperatures. However, we now realise that the other side of the coin was also equally uncomfortable. We found the room temperature in the hotel was too cold.

We couldn't work out how to control the temperature level, so we got in touch with hotel officials. They informed us that the entire hotel was centrally air-conditioned, and it was impossible to control the temperature in a particular room. One person suggested that keeping the window open would raise the room temperature.

We had three days before the ship was due to sail on 22 June 1972. So we decided to go on a sightseeing trip to enjoy the soothing green scenery of Cochin.

Whenever we were out together, onlookers were curious about us. We were always in uniforms, and once they read the sign, 'World Tourist Bangladesh', they would stop and ask us questions about the liberation war. Sometimes we were drawn into lengthy conversations. On the first day, while we were going around the coastal area of Cochin and enjoying the natural beauty, a gentleman approached us. He introduced himself as an active member of the Cochin Rotary Club. He told us that the people of Cochin knew of the Bangladeshi cyclists who were touring India. He informed us that he would ask the Rotary Club committee to invite us to a reception so that other members could meet us. We thanked the gentleman but expressed our doubts. We explained that we were leaving Cochin in three days. The gentleman made a note of our hotel and later came to see us. He said the Cochin Rotary Club was due to meet the day before we left, and they had already squeezed us into their regular meeting. We were happy to have the opportunity of meeting the Rotarians at such short notice.

ROTARY CLUB OF COCHIN

Meeting No. 51.
Date: 21-6-1972.

ORDER OF BUSINESS

6.30 P.M.	1. Meeting called to order	: By Rtn. Pres. M.M. Abdul Khader
	2. Introduction of Visiting Rotarians	: By Rtn. Pres. M.M. Abdul Khader
	3. Introduction of Guests	: By Members
	4. International Toast	: By Rtn. L. Vishnudas.
	5. Birthday Felicitations	: By Rtn. Rajkumar.
	6. Introduction of Bangla Desh Youths	: By Rtn. K.V. Mathew
	7. Reply	: By Head of the Delegation.
	8. Introduction of Chief Guest/Speaker	: By Rtn.PP. Dr. V.B. Muhamed.
	9. Speech	: By Dr. Sivadas, M.Sc. Ph.D.
	Subject	: "LACCADIVE ISLANDS"
	10. Questions	: By Members
	11. Vote of Thanks	: By Rtn. K. Narayanaswamy.

****

KOB/

A copy of the Cochin Rotary Club's order of business

At the reception, speakers thanked us for attending their meeting at short notice. They expressed their happiness that we had won the war. We conveyed our Prime Minister's greetings and expressed our gratitude to them. We thanked the audience, the people of India, and those elsewhere who had supported our cause. We stressed that our victory was not only for the Bangladeshi people but for freedom lovers worldwide.

On 22 June 1972, we set off for the port, only a mile away from the hotel. We were surprised to see a big crowd boarding the ship. We had not expected to see so many people boarding a cargo ship. One member of the ship's crew approached us and helped us to jump the queue, saying, 'The captain and the chief officer are waiting for you.'

SEVENTEEN

THE VOYAGE: On board Bishva Prabha

None of us had ever been on an oceangoing ship. Our experience of travelling by water was limited to short trips by small passenger boats, journeys by small rowing boats in the canals, or river trips on a launch. However, journeys by boat or launch have always been a pleasure. Therefore, our expectations of an exciting sea voyage were extremely high.

As we climbed the gangway to board the ship, people observed us with amusement, noticing the four of us in uniforms and each carrying a bicycle. Once on board the boat, we realised a party was going on. The captain was in conversation with a few people. Then, seeing us, he excused himself and approached us with a broad smile. 'Welcome on board the Bishva Prabha.' He shook our hands, introduced himself as Mr Palmer and introduced the Chief Officer, Mr Nayak, to us. 'Welcome aboard. I hope you will have a pleasant trip with us.'

Neither Mr Palmer nor Mr Nayak looked like typical Indians. Both of them had fair skin and looked European. Mr Palmer was tall, nearly six foot, and Mr Nayak was relatively short, with a slim moustache. We guessed that Mr Palmer must be an Anglo-Indian.

Mr Palmer asked a cadet to take us to our cabins and

invited us to join the party after we left our bikes and luggage in the cabins. On the way to our cabins, we learned that the cadet's name was Karnarou. He was slightly younger than us. Karnarou took us to our cabins and then left for the party. He reminded us not to be late.

We dumped our stuff in the cabin and hurriedly got ready for the party. Initially, we could not find our way to the party. Eventually, we followed the noise and the sound of music and somehow managed to get there.

We were surprised by the quality and amount of food and drink. There was a festive atmosphere, and everybody was enjoying themselves. Later, the captain explained that in the past, a bon voyage party would have been a sombre affair; people would come to the ship to say goodbye to loved ones who would be making a long and potentially hazardous journey at sea. The feeling of separation would have made both the travellers and their close ones feel sad. However, nowadays, travelling by sea is no longer a risky mode of transport. For this reason, embarkation is no longer a sad occasion, it has become a celebration.

After the party was over and the guests got off the ship, it was time for our month-long journey at sea to begin. The vessel blew a few prolonged blasts on the horn, departed from the port slowly and moved towards the deep sea. Naturally, the captain and the crew became extremely busy navigating the colossal ship. We, on the other hand, settled on the open upper deck to observe the big ship moving out of port.

When I saw the whole ship from the shore before we boarded, I was astounded by the enormity of the vessel. And once I was on board, I felt I needed a map or a guide to move around, as I could easily get lost.

The ship started moving steadily; we were in open water, and there was no need for constant manoeuvring. The captain left the bridge and came to get properly acquainted with us. 'I know about all of you as a group, since your stories started appearing in the newspapers. Now tell me who is who.'

We introduced ourselves and thanked him for welcoming us to his kingdom. Then the captain wanted to know if any of us had had the experience of being on an oceangoing ship. We replied in unison, 'No. This is the first time. The captain smiled and said, 'In that case, you have not had the experience of being seasick!' None of us had thought of seasickness. Mentioning this word made us worried. The captain, however, was still smiling and assured us, 'Not everyone gets seasick. In any case, I will ask one of the deck cadets to give you some tablets if you feel uncomfortable. The good news is that on a calm sea, as it is now, you will not feel uncomfortable at all.'

I did not move my focus from the shore until it slowly disappeared and completely vanished. Then I felt that I was not in touch with the ground anymore. I felt like I was floating, without control over myself. I looked around, and the view in every direction gave me the same picture – endless water as far as I could see, all the way to the horizon. It was getting dark; the stars did not show up to brighten the sky, and the atmosphere triggered a hint of depression. Finally, I decided to leave the open deck and find my friends inside.

Later the deck cadet, Karnarou, came to our cabin with the

tablets for seasickness. He told us that dinner would be served at eight o'clock sharp. We asked him to come back to escort us to the dining room as we did not know how to find it.

The captain's table was almost full. Karnarou showed us four chairs and said we would be sitting in these seats every day. An officer nearby commented, 'No musical chairs!' I looked at him and smiled to acknowledge his witty remark. We then looked around the big table and said hello to everybody.

The captain, his wife and their 7-year-old daughter, Pinkie, and the chief officer and his wife entered the dining room and took their seats. The captain welcomed us and introduced us to the rest of the officers, who had not had the chance to meet us formally. The captain then explained that we would meet the rest of the officers later; at that time, they were still on duty. We introduced ourselves to everybody, and everybody warmly welcomed us. The menu was mouth-watering. When the dinner was served, we thought we would be putting on extra weight by consuming such delicious food day after day without doing any physical exercise.

As the days passed, we got acquainted with most of the crew members. But we formed a close relationship with three people in particular: the master of the ship, Mr Palmer; the chief officer, Mr Nayak; and the deck cadet, Karnarou. Karnarou. Karnarou spent most of his free time with us. However, duty hours on the ship did not remain the same. It was neither a day nor a night shift but the most irregular working hours.

One day, Karnarou gave us a guided tour of the ship. I

was pleased to see a table tennis table in their games room. I immediately asked Karnarou if anyone on the ship played the game.

'Do you know how to play table tennis?' Karnarou asked enthusiastically.

'Do I know how to play table tennis? Table tennis is one of my favourite games!'

'You must be very good at this game, then. Unfortunately, I don't think there is anyone on the crew interested in the game. I will give you a game before starting my duty this evening.'

'That would be great. I love this game but am not that good at it. However, I look forward to having a go this evening.'

I realised that being the only player on the ship, Karnarou hoped to impress me with his skill at the game and took me as a novice. He insisted that I play a game rather than carry on practising. After losing a few games, he realised I was too good for him. When I saw how disappointed he was, I explained that I had been the table tennis champion in my college and university hall. This made him happy; he was not losing to a novice. After this, Karnarou and I played table tennis whenever he had free time.

Breakfast, lunch and dinner were the most exciting times because everybody at the dining table would be relaxed and engaged in humorous conversation. The captain and the crew appeared to be members of one happy family. But the most interesting observation for us was the Chief Officer constantly giving Karnarou a hard time. Sometimes Karnarou felt humiliated, and we felt sad for him. I then remembered why the seniors bully the juniors in the army.

While at university, I joined the UOTC (University Officers Training Corps), an Army Reserve unit that recruits exclusively from university students. The aim was to train future generations of officers for the Regulars and Reserves. I never wanted to join the army; I joined the UOTC for fun and for the weeklong camping trip I heard about from the senior students. While in the UOTC, I noticed that it was common for the seniors to bully the juniors, and we felt the army language to be rough and off-putting.

In one of the UOTC camping, one evening, hearing the loud noise of a party, the captain came to our tent. We drew him into a friendly conversation. We asked him to explain why the army had to use foul language so often. For example, why does the army use the word 'bloody' in almost every sentence? The captain explained that this word has no bad connotations in the army. He also explained that bullying is part of army training, to equip the juniors to listen to the seniors without question.

One of us asked the captain, 'If we say, you bloody captain, get lost, will that have any bad consequence?' The captain smiled and said, 'You will be put to death at once.'

Poor Karnarou had no option but to endure this humiliating treatment until he finished his training. The irony was that once he became a senior officer, he would be bullying his juniors.

While in India, I wrote to my close a friend, Sohrab, that

we would likely go to Europe by ship. Sohrab, wrote back, informing me how enjoyable a journey it would be.

Sohrab was so right. It did not take long to discover the beauty of the sea. Besides having the opportunity to breathe pure air, the sea opened my eyes to the wonders of nature. I felt so humbled seeing the enormity of the majestic ocean, which forced me to realise how insignificant we were in comparison.

I found it genuinely fascinating to sit alone under an overcast sky and gaze out over the endless expanse of water, which did not seem to have any boundaries. Whenever I got bored, I went to the upper deck to enjoy listening to the gentle sound of the mild wind and watching the gentle movement of water, which sounded like soft music. When the sea was calm, and there were no wild waves or storms, I discovered that the seawater never went to sleep, like the water in a swimming pool. Underneath the surface, the water was always in movement, never still. The movement of the water seemed to be quite mystical. I discovered the pattern of the swell, which gave me the feeling that something or somebody was pushing the water up in one area and pulling it down in another. Slowly I began to imagine that someone, perhaps a mermaid or a lustful young lady, was being carefully careless in maintaining her modesty with inadequate clothes. She was pulling her clothes to cover the exposed part of her body, and while doing so, she was exposing another part, making her try to adjust her dress immediately. This endless attempt to adjust her clothing appeared to be causing the movement of the water, which

I found alluring, and it kept me focused on the mystifying motion of the water.

After looking at the sea for some time, I developed another vision. I felt like I was looking at a moving abstract display of a great artist's work. Just as different people always have different interpretations of an abstract painting, I knew that what I was seeing, or rather imagining, from the display of the fascinating water would most likely not be seen or felt by another person. However, watching the water movement, I formed an imaginary description, which I shared with my friend, Sohrab in Bangladesh, who had told me that a journey by ship would be fascinating.

My friend wrote back saying that he found my expression of the movement of the seawater so interesting that he had shared a particular section of my letter with some of his friends.

While on the bridge, the captain would invite me to talk whenever he was free. The captain used to call me 'Captain'. Once, he said at the dining table, 'We have two captains on the ship!' I found the captain very knowledgeable and always happy to explain things on many subjects, particularly about the ship and sea life.

One day the captain explained why the captain of a ship is also popularly called the 'master' of the ship. He explained that 'captain' is a rank in the armed services (Army, Navy and Air Force), but it is only a courtesy title in the merchant navy. In the merchant navy, the person in charge, with ultimate responsibility for the vessel's command, is the shipmaster, who is not a member of the crew but the representative of the ship's owner. For this reason, the captain is known as the master of the vessel. The crew's ranks were the chief officer, also known as chief mate, then second mate, third mate and deck cadets. These people were responsible for the navigation of the ship. The other crew members were the chief engineer, second engineer, third engineer etc., who were responsible for ensuring the smooth running of the engine. In the old days, all ships were steam-powered, burning coal. However, since the 1950s, coal-fired engines have become obsolete, and oil has emerged as a cheaper, cleaner and less bulky alternative.

Bishva Prabha was not a passenger ship, but it was not an unimpressive and ugly-looking tanker either. A structure occupying a small part in the middle of the vast upper deck consisted of a bridge at the top (the room where the ship is navigated) and three floors underneath the bridge to accommodate the ship's crew; it all looked quite impressive.

Unlike on a passenger ship, where the open deck houses a swimming pool surrounded by sun-bathing beds, Bishva Prabha's open terrace, like any other cargo ship, was mainly used to house the equipment for loading and unloading goods. Nevertheless, the open deck was quite pleasant, with railing and an unobstructed sea view.

One day, the chief engineer offered to give us a guided tour of the engine room. We couldn't believe what we saw and the noise we heard. Everybody in the engine room had to talk at the top of their voices. The noise level in the engine room was thunderous, and it was also very hot. The chief engineer gave a synopsis of the machinery and how those pieces of machinery made the huge ship move smoothly.

The news of a party signalled an escape from the monotonous routine. Was it someone's birthday? We wondered. Karnarou explained that the crew celebrates when a ship crosses the Equator. I was surprised and said that the Equator was an imaginary line. How could you ever see or determine this in the middle of the sea? Karnarou replied like an expert, 'We know this sort of thing! By the way, it is not going to be an ordinary party. Just wait and see.'

The next time I saw the captain, I asked him about this forthcoming party. He gave me a mysterious smile and said, 'Don't worry. We will be kind to you people. You are our guests.' The captain's remark made me more curious. After my insistence, he explained, 'We will cross the line of the Equator next week. It has been a long-established ritual for sailors to mark the line-crossing event. This line-crossing ritual goes back hundreds of years.' After taking a short pause, Mr Palmer continued, 'The line-crossing ritual was an initiation service for the sailors who had not yet crossed the Equator. In the past, all sailors who had never crossed the Equator before would be treated as novices, popularly known as 'pollywogs' (baby frogs or toads), and they would have to go through an initiation ordeal when crossing the Equator. They had to pass certain tests in the initiation to prove they could handle rough times at sea. In the past, it was the practice not to accept a sailor as a trustworthy seasoned seaman until he had crossed the Equator.' The ceremony was about a mariner's transformation from a novice to an expert sailor. 'In the nineteenth century and earlier, the ceremony was brutal, often involving beating the pollywogs with wet ropes and throwing the victims over the side. After several pollywogs were killed, most countries imposed restrictions.

Gradually the cruel treatment became harmless entertainment for the senior sailors.

'In the past, the line-crossing ceremonies would start with a beauty contest, when the men would dress up in women's clothes. At some point, the pollywogs would be required to appear before the court of King Neptune. Senior sailors would bring charges against the pollywogs and interrogate them. The senior sailors would always find the pollywogs guilty as charged. The pollywogs would then be punished. They would have to undergo several embarrassing ordeals to entertain the senior sailors before they would be accepted as the sons and daughters of King Neptune.'

I could feel that Mr Palmer was revisiting his early sea life. Maybe he remembered when he was a pollywog and first crossed the Equator. When he took a long pause, I asked him to explain how King Neptune, from Greek mythology, got involved with this ceremony.

'King Neptune is not from Greek mythology, Mr Palmer corrected me. 'In Greek mythology, they have a sea god known as Poseidon. King Neptune is the sea god from ancient Roman mythology. Like Greek mythology, Roman mythology is also very interesting, particularly the story of King Neptune and the sea goddess Salacia. She was the female divinity of the sea who presided over the ocean's depths.' Noticing my interest in such stories, he continued.

'According to Roman mythology, Salacia was the consort of King Neptune. Salacia was described as the most beautiful maiden. However, Salacia was nervous and scared to marry a powerful king. She escaped from him, hid in the deep Atlantic Ocean and continuously moved from one end to the other end of the ocean so that King Neptune could not find her. Finally, he sent a dolphin to find Salacia and make her agree to marry him. After the dolphin persuaded Salacia to marry King Neptune, it was given a place in heaven.'

The next day when I was looking at the sea, the captain's description of Queen Salacia appeared in my imagination. It was no longer an ordinary beautiful young woman adjusting her clothes; I felt the beautiful Salacia driving her pearl shell chariot drawn by sea horses. Her short robe was flying like a kite in the wild wind, and she was trying to maintain her modesty with one hand while controlling the chariot by pulling its harness with the other hand.

On the day of the party, Karnarou and other junior officers got busy decorating the dining room. Music was playing, and food and drink were being served. As the captain had previously told me that the nature of this party had changed to that of a typical harmless celebration, I was pleased not to see any frightened pollywogs waiting to be punished by the senior sailors. However, I was startled when one officer got the attention of everybody and introduced the captain as King Neptune! Here we go, I thought. The officer continued that King Neptune would hear the charges against the accused (though no mention of 'pollywogs') and give his judgement.

When the announcer was detailing the court's orders, the chief officer shouted, out of nowhere, 'Karnarou, tell us a joke.'

Poor Karnarou replied without making eye contact with the chief officer, 'I do not know any joke, Sir.'

'OK. Sing a song.'

'I cannot sing either, Sir.'

'You bastard', the chief officer shouted. 'I asked you to sing a song. So you better start singing.'

Karnarou knew that the chief officer would not spare him. So he hummed a few lines of a song that sounded like a recitation.

The captain rescued Karnarou and banged his table to stop everybody from laughing at Karnarou. Then he said, 'On a serious note, I must inform everybody that someone has been stealing my cigarettes. Will the culprit confess?' Everybody was looking at each other, and after a while, the Spark (radio officer) stood up and said, 'Strictly speaking, it was not stealing. I bought the cigarettes and made the necessary payment.'

'What do you mean? Whom did you pay?' shouted King Neptune.

'I always gave chocolates to your daughter to supply the cigarettes.' Everybody started to laugh and shouted, 'Not guilty. Not guilty.' The captain also smiled and said, 'That is another crime, corrupting my daughter!'

To our great surprise, the chief engineer stood up and brought a charge against us. 'The cyclists claim that the speed of our ship is too slow and that they can ride their bikes faster!'

Everybody appeared shocked. 'How dare the cyclists make such offensive remarks?' Then everybody cried, 'They are guilty and must be severely punished.'

We looked at each other. I was not sure that any of us had ever made such comments, but the senior officers would always have their way in King Neptune's court. There was no chance of success of a 'not guilty plea. The captain looked at me and said, 'Captain, as a punishment, you have to perform to entertain us.'

I found myself in an awkward position. Neither I nor any of us was able to perform. Then suddenly, Akhtar ran to the captain and whispered, loudly enough so that most of us could hear, 'Our captain can play the flute.'

'Excellent!' The captain asked Akhtar to get the flute. The next second, Akhtar left the party and returned quickly with my flute.

The captain addressed the court. 'It has been decided that the cycling team captain will play his flute as their punishment.'

I got up and pleaded to be excused. 'I have never performed in public because I cannot really play the flute. I can hardly make a noise on this thing.'

'We are not interested to hear anything except a nice tune coming out of your flute.' The captain was adamant.

What an embarrassing situation it was. I didn't know what to do, but the captain did not want to wait much longer. So he asked everybody to keep clapping until I started playing the flute.

I realised that there was no way I could get away without

playing the flute, however poor my performance was. Then I struggled to choose a song. I could play only a few lines from limited Bengali songs. As nothing came to my mind, I attempted to play a few lines from our national anthem. Before it became our national anthem only a few months earlier, it had always been a popular and appealing Tagore song for the Bengalis. It is about praising mother Bengal. The English translation of the first few lines is as follows:

My golden Bengal, I love you.
Forever thy skies, thy air set my heart in tune as if it were a flute,
O, mother! The aroma of the mango orchard in Falgun drives me crazy,
Ah, what a thrill! And how dear Bengal is all over the world.

When I started playing the flute, I could feel the festive and joyous party atmosphere turn sombre; the song was most inappropriate for a party.

I had to explain that it was a popular Tagore song that had just become our national anthem. I took the opportunity to remind everybody that, like India, who chose one of Tagore's songs as their national anthem, we also honoured Tagore by choosing one of his songs as our national anthem. I then looked at everybody to see their reaction and was pleased to see the captain start to applaud, and everybody followed him. I thanked God for saving me from embarrassment.

The party went on until late, and we all thoroughly

enjoyed the pleasant break from the monotonous routine of life.

After the party was over, we went back to our usual routine. We strictly followed the time of breakfast, lunch and dinner and presented ourselves at the dining table without having to apologise for being late.

Karnarou had been fantastic, helping us not to get bored. He hardly had any free time as, after his duty hours, he would spend most of his time playing card games or table tennis or just gossiping with us. Whenever he visited us in our cabin, he would bring some food. One day he confessed to us that, when they were loading cargo in Cochin port, he had set aside a sizeable container of cashew nuts. It must have been an open secret as he shared his nuts with almost everybody. We also realised that he had a good relationship with the kitchen staff; they often gave him food, and he would share it with us.

Akhtar became seasick soon after the ship entered deeper waters. We saw the second officer, also known as the medical officer. He advised Akhtar to drink plenty of water and divert his mind. He also advised him to sit facing the direction we were moving. The medical officer also advised us to keep our eyes on the horizon. However, it took nearly a week before Akhtar recovered from his sickness.

One day Karnarou made us feel sad when he said, 'After you get off in Athens, the rest of the voyage will be boring for me.' We shared his sadness and said that this long journey would have been so dull for us without his company. We would remember the fun time we had for a long time.

Soon after we passed the Equator, Akhtar became ill again. One of his hands somehow got poisoned, and he was in severe pain. The second mate was unable to prescribe any medication. The captain got in touch with the Shipping Corporation in India. The shipping corporation advised him to delay our stay in Las Palmas so Akhtar could receive medical treatment.

The original plan had been to stop at Las Palmas only for re-fuelling. However, because of Akhtar's illness, we were allowed to get off the ship and enjoy the experience of this small, picturesque island. Everybody was dying to get off the ship, at least for a few hours. Having spent weeks at sea, we were thrilled to walk on the land. Las Palmas is a beautiful island with exotic flowers all around. However, it is hilly. It was not a smooth and relaxed walkabout. However, this did not stop us from roaming around, climbing up and down the unfriendly walkways. We spent all our energy exploring the island. We thought we were in heaven. The other thing that made the island so attractive was the sound of melodic songs from everywhere. We did not understand a word of the language that the people on the island were speaking, but it sounded so pleasant. Later we learnt that Las Palmas was a Spanish island.

Poor Akhtar missed all the fun and excitement on the island as he was taken to a hospital. We visited him in the hospital to cheer him up. The captain and the chief officers' wives also visited him to thank him. 'Because, of you, we have been able to have such a nice time on this island!'

Strolling on the island for a few hours refreshed us and helped to recharge our run-down bodies and minds.

Soon after leaving Las Palmas, we entered the Mediterranean Sea, which greeted us with a dazzling blue sheen. We were excited but, at the same time, a bit nervous about facing Europe. Firstly, we worried about communicating, as we did not know any European languages, and the Europeans might not speak English, the only language we could talk and understand a little bit.

Finally, on 3 August 1972, we woke up early and got ourselves ready to embrace Europe. Naturally, as soon we saw the shoreline, we became excited. But at the same time, we became nervous; besides the language problem, our journey in Europe might not be as smooth as in India. Moreover, we were concerned that, what with the different climates and cultures, God knew what else would make our tour in Europe a difficult one.

Bishva Prabha did not dock directly in Piraeus but anchored very close to the docking area. After a while, the port pilot on a small boat came aboard the ship to fetch us. An agent of the Shipping Corporation of India and an immigration officer accompanied him. The captain handed us over to the shipping agent and said, 'You are in good hands. This gentleman will look after you during your stay in Athens.'

Shipping Corporation of India gave us a copy of their letter to the Greek immigration authority. The captain informed me that the Greek authorities had already received the letter, and it was unnecessary to produce documents except for our passports.

To our surprise, the immigration officer quickly finished all the formalities and allowed us into Greece.

Before we got off the ship, it was a sad scene on board. All the crew members assembled to bid us goodbye. We profoundly thanked everybody for looking after us so well. We all became emotional and found it difficult to say goodbye properly. The captain and the chief officer wished us the best of luck. Karnarou could not hide his tears. We hugged him one by one and thanked him for giving us the most enjoyable time during the month-long journey.

EIGHTEEN

Athens

As soon as we got off the pilot's boat and put our feet on Greek soil, I was overwhelmed, remembering the thousands of years of ancient history and civilisation. It was strange that our background knowledge of this most exciting country, however limited, reminded us of many events that happened here in ancient times.

We were relieved that we did not have difficulties communicating with anyone in English, as the people in the port area spoke it fluently.

The first thing that came to mind was that it was in Greece where the theory of democracy was first developed and practised. However, it was disappointing that from 1967, Greece moved away from democracy and had been under army rule. Fortunately, however, about a year after leaving Greece, we learned that Greece returned to democracy in 1973.

The other famous export of Greece to the whole world has undoubtedly been the Olympic Games. The world remembers Greece's glorious past every four years because these games originated in Greece Olympia nearly 3,000 years ago.

In Piraeus, I did not want to indulge in remembering too much about ancient Greece, as I would have enough time to see the marks of this country's glorious past when I visited the tourist attractions later. However, I thought it most appropriate to focus on most recent cultural export from Greece while I was in the port.

It was a song that had taken the whole world by storm. It was from the movie called, '*Never on a Sunday* (Greek name, 'Ta Pediá tou Pireá', meaning 'The Children of Piraeus'). The title song, 'Never on a Sunday', won the first Foreign Language Academy Award for Best Original Song in 1960. The title song of this film became so popular that it was translated into over twenty languages. Many famous artists all over the world recorded this song in their language. I still remember listening to it as a teen while living in Bangladesh, playing it on my mouth organ.

While we were still in the port, the agent gave us our mail, which had been forwarded to him by the Shipping Corporation of India. Receiving the letters, we were so excited that we wished we could go through them immediately. But we resisted the temptation, as the agent still had important information to give us. First, he gave us good news. He told us he had arranged our accommodation in a hostel for athletes near the Olympic stadium. He told us that we could stay there during our stay in Athens. We were so engrossed with the events that we forgot to think about how we would find our accommodation. We also forgot to be concerned about how we would cope with this problem in a foreign country.

I noticed that Akhtar had quietly moved away from us. He could not wait to know how his wife, our Dilara *bhabi,* and their newly born daughter, Lita, were doing. Akhtar quickly read his wife's letter and joined us with a happy face, knowing his wife and daughter were okay.

The agent gave us the hostel's address and directions. He also gave us the address of the Ministry of Tourism and advised us to visit their office for any help. Finally, he told us that he had contacted a cycling organisation in Athens and they would meet us soon.

The agent gave us his contact details and asked us to contact him whenever needed. We thanked him and headed toward our hostel. We felt fortunate to have the accommodation pre-arranged for us. We realised that it must have been the Shipping Corporation of India who had made this specific request to their agent. We remember the Shipping Corporation of India with our sincere gratitude.

Once on the street, we were alarmed to discover that people were driving on the right. We rode our bikes slowly and enjoyed the eye-catching Greek capital. Athens appeared attractive in many ways; firstly, the city was not noisy, like Bangladesh and India. Secondly, we found Athens extraordinarily bright and clean, and the air quality seemed pure.

The hostel was not far from the city centre. It did not take long to reach it. The opportunity of staying in this unique hostel, where Olympians from many countries stayed in the past, gave us a thrill.

Soon after we reached the hostel, we had three visitors. These three were members of the local cyclist club (SEGAS). They were riding their fancy racing bikes with gloves and hats on. Seeing our bulky traditional cycles, they were surprised that we did not have the proper equipment. After we explained the purpose of our tour was not a race but a special goodwill mission on behalf of our country, they became interested to know more about our tour, particularly how we were coping with everything. We informed them that we had been fortunate to receive help and support from everybody concerned. We showed them some newspaper cuttings about the tour. The cyclists became very interested to know how they could help us.

Three cyclist friends from the local cycle club

We told them that the first thing on our minds was to see a journalist in Athens. We wanted to publicise the fact that we had arrived here from Bangladesh to convey the good wishes of the father of the nation and the people of Bangladesh to the people of Greece. We also wished to see the Prime Minister and said we would be grateful if they could show us how to get to the Prime Minister's office. The other thing they could help us with was to take us to the Olympic stadium.

Our new friends were extremely helpful and agreed to take us to a newspaper office immediately and then direct us to the Prime Minister's Office. They told us we could see the Olympic stadium, which was only a few minutes' walks from our hostel, in the late afternoon. So our three friends asked us to follow them on our bikes. They took us to a newspaper office and told us they would drop in to our hostel later to take us to the Olympic stadium.

The journalist was surprised to see us in uniform arriving at the office on our bikes. We introduced ourselves and showed him various documents and photographs of our tour. We explained that we would like him to pass the good wishes of our Prime Minister and the people of Bangladesh to the people of Greece. After that, the journalist became interested to know more about us. He told us that our story would be published in his newspaper shortly.

After finishing our interview with the journalist, we hurriedly returned to the hostel, as our cyclist friends would be coming to see us.

Our three cyclist friends were waiting for us. We were so eager to see the stadium that we suggested we go there immediately and talk when we got there. They thought it was a good idea and led the way.

Inside the Athens Olympic Stadium

Akhtar and I could not resist and ran at the Athens Olympic Stadium!

Once inside the stadium, we were stunned to see this most beautiful stadium, made of white marble. Later we learned that no other stadium was fully made of marble. We all felt excited to be inside the historic stadium.

Our friends gave us the disappointing news that the Olympic Games did not originate here in Athens but in Olympia, over two hundred miles away. All three of them appeared to be fully conversant with the history of the games, and each of them added information when one forgot to mention a particular detail.

We understood that the Olympic Games were initially staged for the local people in Olympia. Later this game became so popular that it spread all over the Greek world. Initially, it was a part of a religious festival and worship of the Greek god Zeus.

In ancient times, before the Olympic Games would start there would be an announcement that no one should engage in war or conflict so that people from all parts of Greece could safely travel to Olympia to participate in the games and religious festivals.

Later, I found out that, after the Romans occupied Greece, they initially respected the Olympic Games, and one of the famous Roman emperors, Nero, even participated. However, the Roman emperors later disapproved of the worship of Zeus. For this reason, they banned the games. As a result, there were no Olympics for nearly 1,500 years.

Finally, a Greek poet and newspaper editor, Soutsos, thought of reviving the Olympics. He published a poignant poem in his newspaper called "Dialogue of the Dead". The poem was about how Plato would have been shocked and distressed to see the present miserable condition of Greece. Plato's ghost deplored the missing marble statues and theatres. The ghost asks the Greek people, 'What happened to glorious Greece, notably the Olympics?' This poem made everybody interested in bringing back the games. Soutsos convinced Greece that the Olympic Games symbolised ancient Greek traditions.

After many years of campaigning to resurrect the Olympics from the buried and forgotten grave, Soutsos found a successful businessman and a philanthropist to fund the enterprise. After 1,500 years, the Olympic Games were born again. However, the games found a new, modern home in Athens instead of settling in its old home in Olympia.

Subsequently, Britain, France and a few other countries joined Greece and founded the International Olympic Committee (IOC).

Since 1896, the Olympics are no longer a Greek affair but have become an international sports festival. The IOC held its first Olympic Games in 1896 in Athens, right on the spot where we were listening to our cycling friends tell us the history.

As time passed, the Olympics Games added new features all the time. The number of athletic events expanded. The modern Olympics have become a festival praising the athletic talents of all the world's nations rather than worshipping the mythological gods and goddesses. However, one original feature of the ancient Olympics, the lighting of the Olympic flame, has been retained, and it too is being developed every year. This ritual continues as a symbol of continuity between the ancient and modern Olympics.

There is a ceremony near the Temple of Hera, at the sacred site of Ancient Olympia, where the Olympic Games originated 3,000 years ago. A series of rituals are performed, and then the high priestess ignites the Olympic flame using the sun's rays and a parabolic mirror. This flame is relayed by torch to the venue where the Olympic Games will be held. The fire stays lit until the games are finished.

The first significant addition to the Olympic Games was in 1920, which saw the introduction of the Olympic Flag with five interlocked rings in five different colours, indicating the five continents of the world and encompassing the colours of the national flags of all the participating countries. Also, the introduction of the winter Olympics in 1924 and the Paralympics in 1960 made these games more interesting.

While most of ancient Greece has become history, the Olympic Games remain one piece of the distant past of Greece that continues as a present-day event. Some 3,000 years after the Olympic Games started, it remains one of the most popular and wonderful events, not just for Greece but, since 1896, for all the nations of the world. There is no sign that the Olympics will be consigned back to history. On the contrary, they will likely continue for thousands of years.

We stayed only a few hundred yards from the stadium, and we decided to revisit the stadium as often as possible.

The next day we set off for the Prime Minister's office. We introduced ourselves and explained that we wished to see the Prime Minister. After a while, a young lady came to see us and informed us that the Prime Minister was not available, but his undersecretary would like to meet us. She led us to the Undersecretary of State, Mr Stamatopoulo's office.

Mr Stamatopoulo was delighted to meet us and had a lengthy conversation about our liberation struggle. He thanked us for the gift of our national flag. He offered us help during our stay in Athens. We expressed our wish to appear on national television to convey the good wishes of the people of Bangladesh to the Greek people. Mr Stamatopoulo looked at his secretary and asked her to arrange for a T.V. interview for us. He then gifted us DM4000 and advised us to approach his secretary, Ms Yulya, for any other help we needed. Ms Yulya took a particular interest in helping us. She took us to her office. She telephoned the T.V. office and made an appointment for us the following day.

Ms Yulya gave us the address of the T.V. station and told us we would be met by someone called Jacob. She then gave us four passes for free entry to various tourist attractions in Athens. In response to her question, we told her we would like to go to Thessaloniki and Yugoslavia. Ms Yulya looked concerned. 'You cannot ride your bikes to Thessaloniki, as the road conditions are not good for cycling.' Noticing our surprised expressions, she explained that the Greek government could not guarantee our security on the three-hundred-mile journey to Thessaloniki by bike. She also explained that frequent terrorist attacks outside Athens made it risky to travel by bicycle. Moreover, the roads were hilly and not suitable for riding bikes. She noticed the disappointment on our faces. However, she continued, 'Do not worry. I will arrange your journey to Thessaloniki by train. Then you can ride your bikes from Thessaloniki to the Yugoslav border. I will also book your accommodation there and make an appointment to see Thessaloniki's Commissioner and Undersecretary of State, Mr Anastasopoulou.

Ms Yulya asked us to see her the day before we left for Thessaloniki. She then invited us to attend an open-air concert that evening. It was a musical. 'I am sure you will enjoy the show.' While she gave us the address for the concert, she told us, 'I will meet you at the entrance, and I will have the admission passes for you with me.' We thanked her. 'We sincerely appreciate your help and cooperation.'

'It was my pleasure. I look forward to seeing you this evening.'

We left the Prime minister's office in a very uplifting, happy mood. We couldn't believe our luck. All our anxiety about our European tour was over. We became optimistic about our prospect of a successful journey in Europe. We then roamed around the city. We were amazed to see the seating areas from the main restaurants spilling out onto the pavements. There were hardly any customers sitting inside the restaurants, and it appeared that everybody preferred to have their lunch outside on the pavement. Seeing people enjoying their lunch, suddenly, we felt hungry and cherished the idea of tasting Greek food while sitting at a table outside on the pavement.

It wasn't easy to choose what to eat. We had never seen breadsticks before, except in French movies. So we decided to order them. We were pleased to see thick slices of cheese and dips made of cucumber and yoghurt were served on the house. After munching the hard bread with cheese and dips, we fancied some grilled meat. Some of us tried Moussaka, which looked tasty. While eating, we missed the traditional Bengali hot, juicy and spicy kabab and salad made of tomatoes, cucumber, onions, hot green chilli and coriander. However, non-spicy Greek food was exciting, and we thoroughly enjoyed the new experience.

After lunch, we returned to the hostel quickly so we could pop into the Olympic stadium again.

In the evening, we returned to the hostel to prepare for the open-air concert. Ms Yulya was already there waiting for us. People were greeting each other, and there was a real hustle and bustle. Yet, at the same time, we could feel calm and tranquillity. It was the most relaxing atmosphere in which to unwind after a hard day. Before the show started, Ms Yulya gave us good news. She told us that she had arranged our accommodation in Thessaloniki and made an appointment to meet Mr Stamatopoulo the day after our arrival.

We enjoyed the beautiful sound of soothing music and the dancers' breathtaking balletic, graceful movements.

The next day we attended the T.V. station for the interview. We were pleasantly surprised when we were greeted by a charming gentleman who appeared to be of African origin. He introduced himself as Jacob and informed us he was the programme producer. Jacob took us to his office. He sent for the presenter of the show, and an attractive lady with a smile on her face entered. After the introduction, the presenter took us to her office.

I took out our press cuttings and other documents describing the purpose of our tour and showing our achievements so far. Then the presenter went through the documents while making a note on her clipboard and asking us a few questions to get our background information.

At the outset, Jacob informed us that it would not be a

live show and the programme would be broadcast later in the evening.

After the presenter introduced us to the imaginary audience, we, as usual, thanked people worldwide who had supported our liberation war and recognised our new nation so quickly. We mentioned that it would have been very difficult to win our liberation without the support and help from various countries. And on behalf of our Prime Minister, Bangabandhu Sheikh Mujibur Rahman and the people of Bangladesh, we thank everybody for their support.

In response to the presenter's question, we mentioned that we had already been to the Olympic Stadium but intended to visit again. Our next plan was to see the Acropolis. We would then like to visit a few museums to see the relics of ancient Greek civilisation, which we heard so much about.

After the show's recording, Jacob offered to take us to the Acropolis. On the way, we found that Jacob was a British citizen and had come to Greece when he got this job as a T.V. producer.

Jacob gave us a brief history of how Athens got its name. According to Greek mythology, there was a fight between the sea god Poseidon and the goddess Athena over the control of Athens. Athena won the battle, and the people changed the name of this city to Athens to honour the goddess. All the temples on the Acropolis were dedicated to Athena.

Jacob gave us a guided tour of the Athens Acropolis

With Jacob at the Acropolis

At Athens Acropolis

Athens was a powerful force in developing and advancing western civilisation. There are traces of this rich and mythical history all around the city.

While we were climbing up the Acropolis, Jacob gave us a running commentary. We felt we were extremely fortunate to have Jacob with us, as he explained everything like a professional guide.

When we climbed to the top of the Acropolis, we could see the whole of Athens. I remember being on the top of Qutub Minar in Delhi, seventy-three metres above sea level. The Acropolis's height was nearly double that of the Qutub Minar. Plus, the view from the Acropolis was clearer because of the unpolluted, bright sky. Besides the vast area of Athens, we could also view the sea.

Jacob explained that in Greek, the word 'Acropolis' meant 'the highest point of the city. For many centuries, the Acropolis served many purposes. It was a home for the kings, a mythical home of the gods, a religious centre, but most importantly, it was a citadel. Because of its prime position, one could detect invaders approaching the city by sea or land.

Pointing out the three temples on the Acropolis, Jacob explained that these were the only three temples that had withstood the bombardments by different invaders at different times and a few earthquakes, which destroyed most of the temples and columns. As a result, only these monuments and a few columns have survived to remind us of the architectural wonders from ancient times.

In the sixth century, the Christians converted the temple

of the Parthenon to a church. And when the Ottoman Turks invaded the city in the fifteenth century, they turned the now-Christian Parthenon into a mosque.

In 1941, when Nazi-occupied Greece, two young men climbed the Acropolis and pulled down the swastika flag. This rebellion was the first act of the fierce Greek resistance movement. Since then, the Greek Presidential Guard has performed a flag-raising and flag-lowering ceremony every Sunday morning and evening.

The Acropolis is the site of one of the earliest known settlements in ancient Greece. It was established at some point in the fourth millennium B.C. The monument retains many of its original architectural features.

In 1806, Lord Elgin sought permission from the Ottoman Sultan to remove some of the marble friezes. These sculptures are still housed in the British Museum. Jacob suggested we should visit some of Athens's museums, where we could see relics of ancient Greece.

The next day, after visiting a few museums, we went to see Ms Yulya. She gave us the train tickets for Thessaloniki and the address of our hotel. We thanked her and said goodbye.

NINETEEN

Thessaloniki

On 7 July 1972, we boarded the train to Thessaloniki. The train journey from Athens to Thessaloniki took nearly five hours and was a new experience. It was the first time we had travelled by broad-gauge train, which was much faster than our narrow-gauged, low-speed trains in Bangladesh.

Thessaloniki is the second-largest city in Greece, an ancient port city. Like any other ancient city, Thessaloniki also has the fingerprints of different rulers at different times, and each one has left evidence of their reign.

The city was founded by a Macedonian king, Kassandros, in 315 BC. King Kassandros did not come from a long line of royalty. His father was a general in Alexander the Great's army and governed Macedonia when Alexander was engaged in expanding his empire in Asia. After Alexander's sudden death, somehow, Kassandros succeeded the kingdom and married Thessaloniki, who happened to be Alexander's half-sister. He named the newly built city after his wife.

Because of its strategic location and its port, it became an important trade hub. After Macedonia's demise, Thessaloniki was ruled first by the Romans and then by the Byzantine and Ottoman empires.

One of the interesting facts about Thessaloniki is the

longstanding diversity of its people and their cultural and religious traditions. In the sixteenth century, Jewish people were the dominant community of this city, with more than 50% of the total population, surpassing the Turkish, Greeks, Bulgarians and Roma. Because its population came from diverse cultural and religious backgrounds, Thessaloniki became famous for various festivals and cultural events. As a result, it became the cultural capital of Greece.

On 8 July 1972, we saw the undersecretary of State, District Commissioner General of Central and Western Macedonia, Mr Anastasopolou. Mr Anastasopolou was delighted to meet us. After we presented him with a decorative flag of Bangladesh, he surprised us by presenting us with their country's national fag.

We found Thessaloniki to be a breath of fresh air. Besides quite a few historical monuments, the ruins of the Roman emperor Galerius' fourth-century palace told us about its glorious past. The dome in the palace has been a church and a mosque at different times, a familiar story! In addition, Thessaloniki's leading university, Aristotle University, is the largest in Greece and, in fact, the whole of the Balkans.

We found it fascinating to stroll on the picturesque and beautiful beach promenade of Thessaloniki.

TWENTY

Yugoslavia

(Now Bosnia and Herzegovina, Croatia, Macedonia, Montenegro, Serbia, Kosovo and Slovenia)

Since we had left India and boarded the ship, we hadn't ridden our bikes for nearly a month and a half. So, when we left Thessaloniki for Belgrade, we were excited to be on the road again. After a month-long rest on the ship and then the train journey from one end to the other of Greece, we would travel by bike from Thessaloniki to London. Our first goal was to ride approximately four hundred miles from Thessaloniki to Belgrade. However, our immediate target was to enter Macedonia and reach a town where we could spend the night. The border was less than one hundred kilometres away.

We noticed something strange when we reached the Yugoslavian border (now Macedonia). The road to Yugoslavia abruptly ended in front of a narrow canal, which looked like a wide drain with shallow water. People drove over the shallow water, which turned out to be less than half a foot deep! We noticed that the canal was very short, so we decided to go to the end of the drain and enter Yugoslavia on dry land. Suddenly, a uniformed officer ran after us and asked us to come back to the canal. Then he asked us to ride our bikes through the water in the canal! Seeing our surprised look, he explained that it was not a drain but a trench filled with disinfectant. Everybody had to pass through this. We apologised for our ignorance and slowly rode our bikes to avoid splashing too much water.

When we entered Macedonia in 1972, it was a part of the Yugoslav Federation. Macedonia did not look like a developed western country. It is a place whose roots run deep in history. It is believed that old European civilisation flourished in Macedonia between 7,000 and 3,500 BC. However, in 547 BC, Macedonia became a vassal state of the ancient Persian Empire. After that, the fate of Macedonia kept on changing like a rollercoaster until 359 BC, when under the reign of Philip II, the Macedonian Kingdom became a powerful force in the region. In 336 BC, when his son, Alexander, became the king of Macedonia at the young age of twenty, he became a very powerful king and quickly earned the title of 'The Great'. He fulfilled his father's objective of conquering the whole of Greece. His next target was to overthrow the Persian Empire. Very quickly, his kingdom became the most powerful in the whole world. During his reign, arts, literature, philosophy and engineering flourished to a new height in the Macedonian region. It is believed that Alexander the Great's tutor, the famous Greek philosopher Aristotle, who laid the foundation of Western philosophy, influenced Alexander to concentrate on advancing civilisation.

After Alexander the Great's premature death, all his generals got busy dividing his empire between themselves and making the country weak again. In 168 BC, the Romans, who eventually conquered most European countries, invaded Macedonia. The Romans absorbed both Greece and Macedonia into the Roman Empire. Then the Ottomans conquered the Balkan countries, including Macedonia.

In 1912-13, the Ottomans lost control over the Balkans, but Macedonia did not achieve its independence. On the contrary, its fate brought the worst consequence for Macedonia; the country was divided between Greece, Serbia and Bulgaria.

In 1918 the Southern Slav people formed a new kingdom which later became Yugoslavia (Land of the Slave). After the Second World War, Marshal Tito abolished the Yugoslavian monarchy and Macedonia was established as a constituent state of Yugoslavia.

Entering Yugoslavia, I thought of the famous Marshal Tito. So, naturally, I was excited at the prospect of meeting this outstanding personality.

The weather was perfect for cycling. We rode until it was dark and stayed in a small town for the night. We were excited about seeing mile after mile of agricultural land. Unfortunately, we did not have the opportunity to see such green agrarian land when we were in Athens. We had always been surrounded by harsh concrete, and as we travelled from Athens to Thessaloniki by train, we missed the experience of biking through the countryside.

Having had a month-long rest on the ship and not having ridden our bikes since we arrived in Thessaloniki, we felt fit and ready to return to our old routine. We reminded ourselves that winter was fast approaching. Nevertheless, we were determined to ride all day, taking a minimum of time for rest. Our next target was the Bangladesh High Commission Office in Belgrade.

One memorable incident stands out for me; it could have had horrific consequences, though we escaped by good luck. One day we were riding for long hours, hardly taking any breaks. Before it got dark, we felt we needed a short break. We found an open space off the main road where we could rest. We were so tired that, one by one, we all nodded off. Suddenly we woke up, hearing loud noises and seeing bright lights. To our shock, we found ourselves surrounded by several trucks. It was otherwise completely dark. We were frightened by the bright light from the headlights of the trucks hitting our eyes. One driver noticed us. He got out of his lorry and approached us to find out who we were and what we were doing there. When we explained that we were resting and went to sleep without realising, the driver told us, 'You are extremely fortunate. One of the trucks could have run over you; you were completely invisible from the driver's seat in the dark.'

We realised that we had picked a truck stop and that countless lorries were approaching to park. The driver was kind enough to guide us towards the nearest town. We always preferred staying in a YMCA or a youth hostel. When a hostel was not available, we stayed in a cheap B&B. However, there were times in small towns when we did not find a youth hostel or B&Bs. In those circumstances, we stayed with families for the night. Most families could offer us a room for the night, but there were occasions when we stayed in a barn.

Fortunately, none of us became ill during our long journey from Thessaloniki to Belgrade. We patted each other on the back to reach the Bangladesh High Commission Office in Belgrade within our targeted time.

Belgrade

13 August 1972

We had heard so much about our ambassador to Yugoslavia, His Excellency Shams Ud Doha, and his colourful achievements in life. He was one of the most flamboyant Bengali figures, but we had never had the opportunity of meeting him in person. We heard that he was a bright, tall, handsome person with an outstanding sports career and army background. He was the captain of Kolkata University's athletics team. He was due to represent All India at the 1948 London Olympics, but due to the Partition of India in 1947, he could not compete. He was the first and might have been the only Bengali to graduate as a Sword of Honour Cadet from the Military Academy in Pakistan. However, his smart move was to contest Pakistan's general election in Rawalpindi on an Awami League ticket. Being a Bengali and contesting an election in a West Pakistan constituency on an Awami League ticket was beyond anyone's imagination.

After the independence of Bangladesh, Mr Doha was appointed the first ambassador to Yugoslavia. Later, he also served as the ambassador to Iran and the High Commissioner to the U.K. Subsequently, he was promoted to minister of foreign affairs.

His Excellency Doha was excited to greet us. He was impressed with our tour and congratulated us on our courage and determination. Doha bhai had a lot of exciting news to give us. First, he informed us that Bangladesh had started issuing passports and that we would be issued four Bangladesh passports immediately by the embassy. Until then, we had been travelling using an A4 size travel document. The following exciting news he gave us was that he would arrange an appointment for us with the Vice President of Yugoslavia. He added that he had wanted to make an appointment with Marshal Tito. Unfortunately, Marshal Tito was unwell and was in the hospital. Finally, Doha bhai gave us the most exciting news that Bangabandhu would be in Geneva for a few weeks to recuperate from his successful operation in London. He added, 'If you want to see Bangabandhu in Geneva, you must hurry up and try to be there as soon as possible.'

Doha bhai arranged our stay in a big house rented by the embassy for the embassy staff. One of his nephews, who was the same age as us, stayed there. He invited his local friends to meet us and threw a big party!

When Doha bhai was taking us to meet the Vice President of Yugoslavia, he told us that Yugoslavia had been at the forefront in supporting our liberation struggle.

The Vice President, Dr Vratusha, was happy to receive us and thanked us for the gift of our national flag to him. On behalf of our Prime Minister and the people of Bangladesh, we expressed our heartiest thanks to the Yugoslav government and the people for supporting our liberation struggle and being a close friend of Bangladesh. The Vice President thanked us for passing on the message of peace. He also passed warmest regards to the government of Bangladesh, giving hope of strengthening relations between the two countries.

The newspaper article following our meeting with the Vice President of Yugoslav was "A Message of Peace", and the Photo caption: 'Anton Vratusha and the Ambassador for Bangladesh in Belgrade in conversation with students from this friendly country.'

The main body of the news reported: *Yesterday, the Vice-President, Dr Anton Vratusha, received a group of students from Bangladesh who cycled all the way from their country on bicycles passing on the message of peace. The four art students started on the 17th (typing error: it should have been the 7th) of April from the country's capital on a journey around the world in the hope of completing their mission within one and a half years. The Vice-President thanked the guests for their visit and as a token of peace. He also gave our warmest regards to the government of Bangladesh, giving hope of strengthening relations between the two countries. The Bangladesh Ambassador in Belgrade, Doha, also attended the event.*

We wished we could stay in Belgrade, the beautiful capital of Yugoslavia, for a few more days. We found the city fascinating and full of life. Belgrade was clean, and the beautiful buildings were so impressive. The people were very friendly and hospitable.

Later, we learned that Yugoslavia's support for Bangladesh was outstanding. When China vetoed the application of Bangladesh for membership in the UNO,

Yugoslavia was one of the four countries, together with the UK, India, and Russia, which made a special request to the UNO to admit Bangladesh as a new member.

Leaving Belgrade, we went to Zagreb, a prominent city in Yugoslavia (now the capital of Croatia). We then headed towards Switzerland.

TWENTY-ONE

Switzerland
Geneva, Bern

In 1972 we did not have a Bangladesh embassy in Switzerland. During our liberation war, Mr Waliur Rahman was the deputy head of the Pakistan embassy in Switzerland. He defected from the Pakistan Government in 1971 and claimed asylum in Switzerland. Before a Bangladesh Embassy was established, Mr Rahman started running the Bangladesh mission from his home.

It was in the evening when we reached Geneva. Mr Rahman was expecting to receive us; His Excellency Doha had informed him about our arrival. Mr Rahman quickly arranged our accommodation at a YMCA hostel and told us that we could see Bangabandhu in the morning.

After the successful operation in London, Bangabandhu accepted an invitation from the Swiss government to stay in Geneva for convalescence. The Swiss government arranged a beautiful resort, La Reserve, on the shore of Lake Geneva for Bangabandhu and his guests, who accompanied him from Bangladesh. Bangabandhu arrived in Geneva on 21 August 1972, and we visited him on 23 August 1972.

Before Bangabandhu arrived in Geneva, his doctors advised him to rest completely.

We found Bangabandhu very weak. However, his illness did not stop him from smiling. Bangabandhu was on the front lawn and greeted us warmly. The first thing he asked us was to tell him how our tour was going.

Bangabandhu going through our albums

We all enthusiastically explained that our tour was going quite smoothly. Except for a few minor incidents, we had no real problems. People from all the countries we visited warmly greeted us. We successfully expressed the good wishes of the people of Bangladesh through T.V., radio and newspaper interviews. In most countries, different organisations gave us a reception at which we conveyed our message and spoke about how grateful we were for their support of our cause. It was a nice feeling for us to see how Bangladesh had become a famous country everywhere.

While answering questions from Bangabandhu, I took out our file containing various paper cuttings and photographs of the tour. Bangabandhu went through the pictures, press cuttings and messages of greetings and good wishes from many dignitaries. Then with a smile, he congratulated us. 'Well done, my boys! Keep up the excellent work.'

Then Bangabandhu asked us about our next move. We said that in Geneva, we would visit the UNO and discuss the issue of Bangladeshis stranded in Pakistan. We would also visit the headquarters of the Red Cross to ask them to provide aid to Bangladesh. Then we would visit Germany.

Bangabandhu going through the press cuttings

Bangabandhu asked us if we were worried that the cold winter would cause a problem for our tour. We said that we were concerned about the winter and had planned to reach London before winter became severe. We planned to pass the winter months in London; we would feel at home there among the sizeable Bangladeshi community.

Bangabandhu had a large and devoted entourage. In addition, some officials, including the Bangladesh Deputy High Commissioner to London, Mr Fateh, a prominent journalist, Mr Abdul Matin and a few close friends from London, accompanied him from London to Geneva.

While Bangabandhu talked to us, he noticed Mr Waliur Rahman. He looked at him and said, 'Oly, are you looking after my boys well?'

Before Mr Rahman could reply, I informed Bangabandhu that Mr Rahman was looking after us very well. He had arranged our accommodation immediately after we arrived in Geneva last evening.

Bangabandhu then asked someone to tell H.E. Humayun Rashid Chowdhury, the Bangladesh ambassador to Germany, to get temporary work permits if we were stuck there due to the winter. I was once again surprised at Bangabandhu's awareness of every little thing!

With a smile, he asked us, 'Are you planning to see the Olympics?' Before we could respond, Bangabandhu asked someone to inform the Bangladesh ambassador in Germany to arrange our trip to the forthcoming Olympics in Munich!

Next, Bangabandhu gave us an envelope containing some money to cover our expenses and said, 'It is nearly lunchtime. Do not leave before having lunch here.'

I remembered the day when we left Bangladesh on 7 April 1972 from his residence in Dhaka, when he did the same thing. An envelope containing money. Bangabandhu's caring nature moved me.

After Bangabandhu excused himself to go inside to rest, we talked to the others. Bangabandhu's eldest son, Kamal, was very close by and was waiting for Bangabandhu to finish the discussion with us. He approached to congratulate me on organising the cycle tour. As I was not up to date with the present political situation in Bangladesh, I asked him to tell me the latest developments. Kamal was so sad to break the news that a new political party, JSD, had been formed by a splinter group from the Chatraleague, and our Siraj bhai was leading this group.

Kamal had a long chat with me about the political situation in Bangladesh. He was younger than me, but we knew each other very well. He gave me information about some of our mutual friends, particularly my younger brother, Abu Musa Hasan. My brother was a year younger than Kamal; however, they were close friends. They studied at Dhaka College and in the same department at Dhaka University. My brother Abu Musa Hasan was active in student politics. He was the General Secretary of the Dhaka City Committee of the Bangladesh Students Union.

Mr Rahman had a lot on his plate, running the Bangladesh mission from his home and looking after the big delegation that accompanied Bangabandhu. Afterwards, he told us that there were enough rooms in the huge villa, and he should have thought of accommodating us there. He asked us if we wished to move out of the hostel. We thanked him. However, we felt it would be better to stay in the hostel. We would remain in Geneva for just one more day, and it was not worth making a move just for one day.

Long dining tables were set on the lawn, and delicious dishes were served for the gathering. We enjoyed the lunch, and particularly the company of so many interesting people. While having lunch prominent Journalist Matin bhai sat at our table. He gave us valuable tips about London life. He told us, 'London is a mega city and most people who arrive there from abroad find it difficult to move around without assistance. It is not unusual for someone to get lost. However, if you have the correct address, it will be very easy to move around in London without asking anybody for directions.'

Matin bhai told us we first had to get a copy of the A-Z, a street map of London. 'However, your main problem will be communicating with others, because neither the local people nor you will understand each other's accents. It will take a few days to get over this problem.'

Matin bhai gave us his London address and asked us to visit him soon after we reached there. A gentleman squeezed in at our table and told us he lived in Bern. He invited us to visit him on the way to Bonn. He was surprised when we informed him that we did not plan to visit Bern. 'I do not believe this. Bern is the capital of Switzerland, and how could you not see Bern when you are in Switzerland?' On his insistence, we agreed to visit Bern and took his address.

After leaving La Reserve, we roamed around Lake Geneva. I looked at the famous fountain on Lake Geneva and was amazed. Until now, we had seen pictures of the fountain and knew this was a prominent landmark of Switzerland.

One hundred and forty metres tall, this fountain, called 'Jet d'Eau' (Water Jet), was one of the tallest fountains in the world. Seeing it in person was exceptional. We thoroughly enjoyed the view of the fountain and all around the lake, which looked as beautiful as a picture postcard.

While wandering around Lake Geneva, we noticed countless headquarters of international organisations close to each other on the lakeshore. We were unaware of so many international organisations based in Switzerland and surrounding lake Geneva. As we walked along the shore and noticed so many unknown international organisations, we had to admit our inadequate knowledge. However, we saw some familiar names, such as the UNO Office, WHO, ILO, and International Red Cross.

Most, if not all, international organisations are based in Switzerland because it is the world's first state to maintain a policy of military neutrality. It has not participated in a foreign war since it established neutrality in 1815. The first international organisation, the International Committee of the Red Cross, was founded in Geneva in 1863. Since then, the number of international organisations based in Switzerland has kept growing. It is believed that, at present, Switzerland houses nearly two hundred international organisations.

We continued rambling around the vast Lake Geneva shoreline, with wide roads, beautiful buildings, colourful flowers, and flower beds all adding to this place's attraction. The more we looked around, the more we enjoyed the eye-catching view. We felt that Lake Geneva was one of the most beautiful places we had seen. Later, we witnessed other natural scenic beauty spots in Switzerland, with mountains, valleys, waterfalls, lakes and abundant greenery. However, I felt the lake and the surrounding view complemented each other, making it the most attractive place in Switzerland. The tall fountain in the lake was the jewel in the crown, making the total view so appealing. No wonder the fountain has become a landmark in Switzerland.

International Committee of the Red Cross

The International Red Cross is the oldest and largest international humanitarian network in the world. In 1859, a Swiss businessman and social activist, Henry Dunant, wrote a book about his horrific war experience. This book inspired the creation of the International Committee of the Red Cross. The book also inspired the creation of The Geneva Convention in the following year. Dunant, along with Frederic Passy became the first recipient of the Nobel Peace Prize in 1901. Henry Dunant was also the founder of the Swiss branch of the Young Men's Christian Association (YMCA).

The Red Cross was founded to protect all human life, irrespective of nationality, race, religious beliefs or political opinion. The main aim was to alleviate human suffering. The symbol of The Red Cross is not a religious symbol. It is, in fact, the reverse of the Swiss flag. However, in 1906, the Ottoman Empire insisted that Muslim countries call this organisation the 'Red Crescent, as the symbol of the cross, is closely associated with Christianity.

On 24 August, we visited the International Committee of the Red Cross (ICRC) to discuss the need for humanitarian aid for war-torn Bangladesh. The Red Cross was sympathetic to the idea of giving generous help to Bangladesh; they had already started to help Bangladesh and would continue to do so until we reached normalcy.

UNO

BANGLADESH TODAY

VOL. II No. 3 — A FORTNIGHTLY NEWS BULLETIN — LONDON, SEPTEMBER 15, 1972

BANGLADESH TODAY

STRANDED BANGALEES

UN Effort for Repatriation Assured

GENEVA, Aug. 25:—The United Nations would try its best for the early repatriation of Bangalees stranded in Pakistan, reports BSS.

This assurance was given by Mr. Erik Jansen, Chief of Cabinet of the office of the Director General of the United Nations Organisation at Geneva to visiting four Dacca University students, who were on a goodwill global tour.

The students during their stay with Mr. Jansen had a long discussion on various matters including the plight of the stranded Bangalees in Pakistan.

'Stranded Bangalees: UN Effort for Repatriation assured' is a reproduction of a news article in Bangladesh Today published on 15 September 1972 from Bangladesh High Commission, London.

On 25 August 1972, we visited the UNO. We were fortunate to meet the chief executive, Eric Jansen. He was pleased to receive a souvenir Bangladesh flag from us and expressed his pleasure that Bangladesh had succeeded in its efforts to become an independent country. We mainly discussed the quick repatriation of Bangladeshis stranded in Pakistan. Mr Jansen assured us that the UNO would try their best to solve this problem as soon as possible.

Meeting Mr Erik Jansen, Chief of Cabinet of the office of the Director General of the UNO

Bern

Just as most people have no firm idea whether Sidney, Melbourne or another city is the capital of Australia, many people also mistakenly assume that Geneva, the most prominent city in Switzerland, is the capital. We were not immune from this confusion. In fact, in 1848, when the Swiss federal state was created, it was decided that the country would have no official capital city so that all the 26 Cantons (Districts/provinces) would be given equal importance. Thus Bern is not named as the capital in the country's constitution; in practice, however, as the parliament, government, and foreign embassies are housed in Bern, it has become the de facto capital of Switzerland.

If we had not met the gentleman from Bern who came to see Bangabandhu, we would not have visited Bern. We never planned to visit. However, he persuaded us by saying, 'After all, it is the capital city of Switzerland. You must visit Bern and please visit me when you are in Bern. I live in the heart of the city'. He gave us his address in Bern, and that's why we changed our itinerary.

Travelling through any part of Switzerland was the most eye-soothing experience because of its natural beauty. Unfortunately, during the cycle tour, we did not have the chance to explore the breathtaking scenery of the Swiss Alps. Many years later, however, I had the opportunity of passing through them. The stunning beauty was beyond my imagination! What fascinated me most were the carefree silver clouds floating underneath us, giving me a feeling that I was looking down at the earth from heaven. There are no major waterfalls in Switzerland, like Niagara and Victoria falls, dropping masses of water from on high with a thunderous noise; instead, countless tiny waterfalls smoothly flowing through the mountains make the atmosphere tranquil. Mysterious mountains, often covered by bright white snow and clouds, make one forget everything else.

It was so easy to find our prospective host's address in Bern. We rang his doorbell. There was no response, so we knocked on his door. We must have banged the doors quite hard to express our frustration because, hearing the noise, an old lady came out from the basement flat. She didn't speak a single word of English. However, she invited us in with a smile and a sincere expression of wishing to help us. She almost dragged us to her apartment as if we were about to miss something. After showing us the settee, she went to another room, brought a crate of beer and asked us to drink. We showed her our bikes and tried to tell her in sign language that we would ride our bikes and could not drink alcohol. The lady excused herself and returned with glasses of cold soft drinks. Then she disappeared again.

Soon after, we heard some noise on the street. We stood up to look through the window. We saw a police officer talking to some people. Still, with a smile, the lady indicated that we should go and talk to the police. She dragged us out of her apartment to meet the police. To our shock, we realised the lady herself had called them. We became annoyed with the lady's odd behaviour and asked the police to explain what was happening. The police officer also did not understand English, making the situation worse. A few people joined the scene, and soon a small crowd had gathered. Finally, one teenage boy came to our rescue. With permission from the police, he asked us what we were looking for. We explained that we were tourists from Bangladesh and had come to see an acquaintance. We realised that the gentleman who invited us to visit him was not at home, and this lady had taken us to her apartment and offered us drinks. Now we were shocked to discover that she had called the police.

The lady, still smiling, explained something to the police and the boy. The boy struggled to tell us that the lady thought we needed help and so called the police to assist us. After the misunderstanding was cleared up, the lady insisted that we go back to her apartment again. We thanked her and excused ourselves, pointing at our watches to explain that we were late and should be on the move. The lady held one of our hands and tried to drag us back to her apartment. We asked the boy to tell the lady to excuse us. After this incident, we agreed that our visit to Bern was not, after all, totally uneventful.

Leaving Bern, we got on our bikes and headed towards Germany, our next stop.

TWENTY-TWO

Bonn, Germany

In 1972, when we visited Germany, the country was divided into two independent countries, East Germany and West Germany.

We reached Bonn, the capital of West Germany, on 4 September 1972. The Bangladesh Ambassador, H.E. Humayun Rashid Chowdhury, and the embassy staff received us warmly. They arranged for us to stay on the embassy premises.

Having visited a few European cities by then, when we entered West Germany, we felt it was pretty different from any other European countries we had been to. It was highly advanced, posh and strictly disciplined. We learned that the U-Bahn (underground railway) was completely computerised. Trains would arrive and depart on time to the accuracy of a second.

I do not remember if we noticed any vending machines in other cities. I found it very convenient to buy various articles from vending machines without having to wait for the shop to open. We also noticed that even the dogs (and not only guide dogs) would stop when the traffic lights turned red. In those days, particularly in Asia, such things were unheard of. I found Bonn so mechanised and orderly that there was no room for emotion or something to be impractical or imperfect. When I was a teenager, I learned that 'made in England' and 'made in Germany' denoted the best quality products, and they were more expensive than those made elsewhere.

As I grew, I realised that Germany also had a rich history in many other areas besides industrial developments. This history has shaped a unique culture of literature, art and philosophy. However, I found it difficult to imagine how the country that had given birth to world-famous composers like Sebastian Bach, Beethoven, Brahms, Strauss, Schuman and many others could turn into a robotic mechanised country. Also, I wondered how a world-famous philosopher, Karl Marx, could conceive revolutionary ideas being born and brought up in Germany. I did not look into the depth of my confusion but guessed that those famous people must have lived and worked long before Germany arrived at this position.

Finding the small Bangladeshi community in Bonn brought us back to familiarity. They were untouched by the West German way of life and maintained the typical Bengali culture. In the last few months, we had focused mainly on the cycle tour and had not realised how much we missed our community life. One embassy staff member invited us for dinner in the evening on the first day we reached the Bangladesh embassy in Bonn. Another member of staff booked us for the following night. Gradually, the staff members made a sort of a rota for entertaining us in their houses – typical Bengali hospitality! I felt we were not alone, but everybody was yearning for community lifeThe staff members became nostalgic for such gatherings and engaged in typical Bangladeshi gossiping sessions. We first tasted 'Uncle Ben's rice in Germany, which we found pretty delicious.

One day, Ambassador Chowdhury invited us to have dinner at his residence, and we enjoyed the evening very much. It was not the favourite dishes, but mainly the gossiping sessions which gave us the most pleasure in Germany. We realised we had missed the spontaneous after-dinner discussions on various topics since we left Ganguly'da and Bannerjee'da in Mumbai.

Because the Bangladeshi community in Bonn was small, everybody knew each other, and they would meet socially in the evening at someone's house. At that time, there were no shops for Bangladeshi spices in Germany. So, the Bangladeshis had to travel to London occasionally, mainly for shopping. Before someone would leave, they would get shopping lists from others.

We were over the moon when HE Chowdhury gave us four VIP tickets to visit the Munich Olympics in 1972. He also told us that he had arranged a place for us to stay with a Bangladeshi national, Mr Mosaraf Hossein, a resident of Munich.

Munich

H.E. Chowdhury kindly gave us an embassy car with a driver to take us from Bonn to Munich and stay with us until we returned to Bonn after seeing the Olympics. Mr Hossain was waiting for us and was delighted to receive us.

Mr Hossain was keen to show us the natural beauty of Munich, particularly the famous parks and gardens. Unfortunately, we had to disappoint him. It would have been interesting to see them, but we were mainly interested in the Olympic Games. Secondly, after a nearly six-hour journey from Bonn, we did not feel like going out that evening. We persuaded Mr Hossain that visiting tourist spots might not be possible.

I asked Mr Hossain to drive through the tourist spots when we went to the Olympics venue every day, but we didn't get out of the car to explore.

The MUNICH Olympics

The Olympics was a major sporting event that we all had dreamt about witnessing in our lifetime. We were excited that our dream was coming true.

It was a different experience and a wonderful feeling to be in the crowd of true international sports enthusiasts of all ages, watching the highest level of performance from the very best athletes in the world. It was not only the top-level performance by the Olympians; the whole environment was so festive that we enjoyed every moment of it. I remembered what our cyclist friends in Athens had told us; it was not just a major sporting event but a festival that people had waited for four years to see. Our experience of being spectators of the Olympics surpassed our expectations.

At the Munich Olympic

Signing of autographs

I vividly remember one football match in the Olympics where one team took a free kick. The ball went into the net through the defence wall, to everybody's utter surprise. After seeing this, we had to take time to work out that one of the attacking players stood in the defence wall, and, at the right time, he jumped up so that the ball could go under his feet! This was the first time we saw such a clever tactic.

As we were wearing our Dhaka University blazers, most people were under the mistaken impression that we were competitors and approached us for our autographs. Our explanations that we were just spectators, like them, did not bring any results, as people did not understand a word of what we said. They sometimes formed a queue to get our autographs! After a while, we realised that the best thing would be to takeoff. Our blazers to avoid this harassment.

We planned to visit Hamburg after seeing the Olympics. Akhtar's older brother lived there. Also, Babul's uncle, Mr Mukhlesur Rahman, had told us to visit one of his business associates, Mr Myers, in Hamburg. Babul had contacted Mr Myers and informed him that we planned to visit. Mr Myers had already received the letter, a copy of which was given to Babul by his uncle. Babul told us that he had met Mr Myers in Bangladesh. Mr Myers had visited Bangladesh on several occasions on business, and Babul's uncle always looked after Mr Myers during his stay in Bangladesh.

When we returned to Bonn from Munich, we heard that Akhtar's older brother had come to see us when we were in

Munich. He left a note for us to visit him in Hamburg as soon as possible.

Mukhlesur Rahman

[redacted]

50, Purana Paltan
Line

Dacca - 2
BANGLADESH.

6th April, 1972.

My dear Mr.Meyer,

It is quite a long time that I have not heard from you. I always remember you with high sense of gratitude and admiration. The man like you impressed me most. The way in which you stand by your friends in distrees is indeed a rare fine in this queer world. Life is still worth living because, there are although a few people like you in the world.

The inevitable has occured. Bangladesh has emerged as a soverign state in its own identity. Loss in terms of life and property during the occupation period was collossal. Devastation to the economy was wide spread and unprecedented. The new nation will therefore be required to put all its to the reconstruction of devastated economy of Bangladesh.

My nephew Mr. M.A. Quayum, bearer of this note together with three of his friends are touring all over the world by bicycle to convey the good wishes of the people of Bangladesh to the people of different countries. They represent the youth of the age, and carry the massage of peace from the suffering humanity of Bangladesh to the peace loving people of other countries. It is an endeavour to gain an insight into the problem of common man, and experience which will stand them in good stead in practical business of living. I shall be deeply grateful if you would kindly extend them all the help and the care they may stand in need of in your great country.

Thanking you,

Sincerly yours,

Mukhlesur Rahman
(MUKHLESUR RAHMAN)

To
Mr. Gerhard Meyer
Gerhard Meyer & Co.,
52, Steindamm
Hamburg 1, West Germany.

Hamburg

When we reached Hamburg, Mr Myers received us warmly. He took us to a hotel and said, 'You are my guests in Hamburg. If you need anything, please do not hesitate to ask.' He was a prominent businessman in Hamburg. We felt fortunate to have a rich, generous, and influential person as our host. We showed Mr Myers some of our press cuttings and expressed our wish to publicise the purpose of our visit to Germany. Mr Myers agreed to help us. He told us that arranging an interview with a newspaper journalist would not be difficult. He also said he would try to make an appointment with the Mayor.

Mr Myers asked his driver to show us the tourist spots in Hamburg. Hamburg is the second-largest city in Germany, the biggest port in Germany, and the third-biggest in Europe. Most of the tourist spots in Hamburg were in and around the harbour. When the driver stopped near an exciting tourist attraction, we got out of the car, only to get back in immediately because of the severe cold. The car's heating was running at full throttle, but we felt numb from the cold. We were nearly frozen. We asked the driver to drive around the huge port area and other tourist spots in Hamburg and then take us back to the hotel.

When we returned to the hotel, Mr Myers informed us that a journalist from a newspaper would see us and that he had already made an appointment with the Mayor of Hamburg.

After browsing our press cuttings and other documents, the journalist expressed his enthusiasm and asked us various questions. We, as usual, expressed our gratitude to the people of Germany for supporting our liberation struggle and for recognising Bangladesh as an independent country.

We had no idea that the Mayor's role and status vary from country to country. In most countries, the Mayor's main duties are to preside at council meetings and to act as ceremonial head of the city. However, the Mayor of Hamburg was quite different. The Mayor, known as Burgermeister (Master of citizens), is the head of government of the city.

Unfortunately, the Mayor, Mr Schulz, had an emergency and was not available to see us. We, therefore, left the gift of our souvenir flag with his secretary. We explained to the secretary that the purpose of our world tour was to thank Germany for supporting our liberation war and for recognising us as an independent nation.

After we returned to Bonn, we received a letter from the Hamburg Mayor's office, which was sent to us by Mr Myers.

Returning to Bonn, we bought some warm clothes (we regretted not thinking of this earlier, mainly before we went to Hamburg).

For unavoidable reasons, Akhtar could not return to Bonn with us. He told us he would be stuck in Hamburg with his brother for a while. He hoped he could join us later, and the best thing would be for us to proceed without him. As we felt that if we did not start our journey soon, we would be stuck, either in Germany or somewhere on the way to Paris, for the whole winter. Therefore, we decided to proceed without him, hoping that he would be able to join us later, maybe in Paris.

FREIE UND HANSESTADT HAMBURG
BEHÖRDE FÜR SCHULE, JUGEND UND BERUFSBILDUNG

STAATSRAT ABEND

Herrn
Jamaz Uddin Md. Hasan

27. Sept. 1972

Herrn
M.A. Quayum

Herrn
Anwaruddin Ahmed

Herrn
Syed Akhter Ali

per Adr.

Herrn
Peter Clasen
in Fa.
Wilhelm G. Clasen

2 Hamburg 1
Glockengießerwall 1

Sehr geehrte Herren,

am 18. September 1972 beehrten Sie mich mit Ihrem Besuch und überreichten mir einen Wimpel mit den Farben Ihrer Nationalflagge. Ich habe Ihr Präsent, entsprechend Ihrem Wunsche, Herrn Ersten Bürgermeister Schulz übergeben und bin von ihm beauftragt worden, Ihnen in seinem Namen aufrichtig zu danken.

Ich komme diesem Auftrag gern nach und bitte Sie, den Dank und die Grüße des Herrn Ersten Bürgermeisters der Freien und Hansestadt Hamburg von mir entgegenzunehmen.

SITZ: 2 HAMBURG 76, HAMBURGER STRASSE 31, FERNSPRECHER: 2 91 88-1

Z 7 5000 7.71 HW

TRANSLATION

From: Freie u. Hansestadt Hamburg
Behörde für Schule, Jugend u. Berufsbildung

27th Sept. 1972

Dear Sirs,

On 18th Sept. 1972 you honoured me with your visit and handed to me a pennant with the colours of your national flag. According to your wish, I gave your present to Burgomaster Schulz and he has instructed me to express his thanks on his behalf.

I do this with pleasure and request you herewith to please accept the thanks and greetings of the Burgomaster of the Free and Hanseatic City of Hamburg.

(sgd)

H.E. Chowdhury gave us a letter of introduction in which he introduced us as the ambassadors of goodwill from Bangladesh.

FEDERAL REPUBLIC OF GERMANY
53 BONN-BAD GODESBERG
KÖLNER STRASSE 54

AMBASSADOR OF THE PEOPLE'S
REPUBLIC OF BANGLADESH

28 September 1972

TO WHOM IT MAY CONCERN

Messrs. Jamal Uddin Md. Hasan, Anwar Uddin Ahmed and Mahmud Abdul Quayum, students of Dacca University, are on a world bicycle tour of goodwill. They have so far travelled extensivaly in India, Greece, Yugoslavia, Italy, Switzerland and West Germany. They are ambassadors of goodwill from Bangladesh and intend to carry the message of goodwill from the people of Bangladesh to the rest of the world. We shall be grateful if they are given all possible courtesies, facilities and help wherever and whenever they stand in need of. The four-member team has now been reduced to a three-member team as the 4th member, Mr. Syed Akter Ali, has to remain behind on account of indisposition, and will join the team shortly.

(H.R. Choudhury)

Early the following day, we left Bonn for Belgium. Soon, we were riding on the autobahn (motorway). Suddenly we were distracted by flashing blue lights and shocked to notice a police car stopping before us, blocking our way. The police asked us question after question about why we were riding bikes on an autobahn. Fortunately, when we explained that we were world tourists from Bangladesh and were unaware that we were not supposed to be on an autobahn with our bikes, the police officers accepted our explanation. Hearing about our destination, they escorted us from the autobahn to a local road and gave us directions toward Belgium. Later we learned that the autobahn was famous for its high speed. Some sections did not have speed limits, and drivers could drive as fast as they wished. Out of curiosity, we asked the police how they had been able to see us. They pointed out a helicopter hovering in the sky and said that all autobahns are controlled by helicopters and other means twenty-four hours a day. The police officer wished us luck. He also told us that the cycling route to Aachen would be a few kilometres shorter than the autobahn, and there we would find the borders of both Belgium and the Netherlands. He also warned us that we might find some parts of the route unfriendly for biking.

The distance from Bonn to Aachen was only sixty miles. However, the first twenty miles were so mountainous that we often had to get off our bikes and walk. Fortunately, after that stretch, the road was not so bad, and we could reach Aachen by the evening.

Reaching Aachen, we needed to find accommodation for the night. We were exhausted from riding on the mountainous road all day and desperately wanted to have a shower. Although Aachen is the meeting place for three countries, we were surprised that the place was not all developed.

Instead of searching for a bed and breakfast, we looked for a big house, expecting to find accommodation for the night. We knocked on the door of a seemingly big house. A man opened the door, and his two children followed him. They were surprised to see three foreigners knocking on their door. They struggled to communicate with us in English.

Before they could articulate their questions, we introduced ourselves and then explained why we had knocked on their door. The father did not understand what we said, but his two sons said, 'Yes. You can stay in our house!' Saying this, they looked at their father for approval. The mother and their oldest daughter had come to the door by this time. They were also surprised to see three strangers. The two sons explained things to their mother and sister. The couple did not want to disappoint their two sons and said, 'Of course, you can stay with us for the night.'

They invited us inside. We realised that the mother and the daughter were about to serve dinner to everyone. She asked her boys to ask us to join them at the dinner table.

We did not realise how hungry we were. To our pleasant surprise, it was not dry bread and cheese but proper food. The sight of roast chicken, boiled cabbage and potatoes made us ravenous. After a tasty dinner, we became so tired that we gave up taking a shower before we went to bed. Instead, we decided to talk to the children and explain the reason for our tour.

Our session with the children was fascinating; the oldest child was much more fluent in English than the boys, and she translated everything for her parents and two brothers.

They asked if they could see photos of the tour and press cuttings.

We had a sound sleep that night. We all had showers before breakfast. After breakfast, we had a photo session in front of our host's house. Finally, we thanked them and said goodbye to this beautiful family and reached the spot where the borders of three countries met and took part in the exciting sport of jumping from one country to another, like all the other tourists.

TWENTY-THREE

With some of our hosts in different countries

During our tour in India and Europe, we stayed at different types of accommodation. In India, we were allowed to stay on the way in government bungalows free of charges. However, when there were no bungalows or bed and breakfast, we stayed with families. In India, there was an incident when we did not find any accommodation available; a police station generously provided us with accommodation. Similarly, in Europe when we did not find hotel, or a big family house to accommodate us, we stayed a night in a barn. In the UK our interesting overnight stay was in priest's family house in Kent.

We fondly remember some of our hosts in different countries, particularly when satisfying the excited children.

With some of our Hosts
In India and Europe

TWENTY-FOUR

Belgium

In September 1972, Bangladesh did not have an embassy in Belgium. However, that was not the reason why we changed our original plan for an extensive tour of this country. The main reason was the severe cold. We decided to ride through Belgium as quickly as possible to reach Paris. Riding bikes wearing overcoats was no fun. We wanted to get to Paris soon as London was not very far from there. Our main aim was to get to London to hole up for the winter.

We had to give up our plan to visit the most important European institutions, the EEC (Now E.U.) and NATO headquarters in Brussels. We also missed seeing the world-famous Belgium chocolate factories!

After visiting Belgium, I learned interesting background information about how Brussels became the de facto capital of the E.U. All six founding member states of the EEC wanted to host the headquarters of this institution in their country. However, failing to decide, the member states agreed to have this institution's head office in alphabetical order for one year. Austria began with A but was not one of the founder members, so Belgium was the country chosen. Brussels became the temporary headquarters of the EEC. Since then, the EEC has been enlarged and renamed from

EEC to E.C. and finally to the E.U., but the temporary base remains in Brussels, perhaps because the European Union doesn't have a capital city. Brussels thus has become the unofficial capital city of the European Union. To date, the E.U. has not been able to decide on a permanent capital or implement its original decision of moving its headquarters every year.

On way to Paris

TWENTY-FIVE

Paris

When we approached Paris, the most talked-about city in the world, we felt the striking difference between Paris and other European cities.

The Bangladesh Ambassador to Paris, H.E. AFM Abdul Fateh, a soft-spoken and scholarly gentleman, welcomed us and introduced us to the third Secretary, Mr Motahar Hossain and told us, 'Mr Hossain will look after you during your stay in Paris.'

Like the Bangladesh embassy in Germany, the Bangladesh embassy in Paris also arranged our stay on the embassy premises.

As we stayed on the embassy premises, we met many interesting and distinguished people visiting Paris's newly established Bangladesh embassy all the time. One such person was Murtuza Bashir, a rising artist in Bangladesh. He was a promising artist and a famous person. Although we had never met Mr Bashir, we had heard of him. We knew he was a son of a famous father, Dr Sahidullah. Dr Sahidullah was the first Muslim PhD holder in undivided India. He was a linguist, philologist, educationist, and writer. Dr Sahidullah was ranked number 16 in the BBC's poll of the greatest Bengalis.

Murtuza Bashir maintained his father's legacy and became an outstanding person in Bangladesh. Though predominantly a painter and known to be a pioneer of surrealist art in Bangladesh, he was also famous for his abstract paintings. He was a poet and author and worked as a researcher, numismatist, and filmmaker.

After graduating from Dhaka Art College in Bangladesh in 1954, he went to Florence to study at the Academy of Arts. Then he studied mosaic and etching in Paris from 1971 to 1973. When we met him in Paris in 1972, he was, therefore, there studying art. He earned several awards for his extraordinarily versatile talent, including Bangladesh's highest civilian honour, the 'Independence Day Award'.

Murtuza Bashir was impressed with our cycle tour. He told us he had some free time and would be delighted to introduce Paris to us. It didn't take long for us to call him Murtuza *bhai* as he became like our older brother. First, Murtuza bhai gave us a lot of information about France, particularly its capital, Paris. Then he told us that France had, and still has, a longstanding status as a centre for art, science and philosophy. Finally, he told us that he would take us to the Louvre, the world's largest art museum, and show us the most exciting places in the city.

Murtuza bhai told us that one needed a long time to explore the Louvre properly. 'The tourists who visit this museum for a short time can only have a superficial view of the massive collection of this huge museum.'

Once we were close to the museum, we were amazed by the building's massive size. Murtuza bhai briefly explained that initially, the Louvre was built as a fortress. Later, it was transformed into a royal palace and, after the French Revolution, the National Museum of France.

Once inside, we felt we had entered a new world. Our idea of a museum was a big building consisting of a few rooms with high ceilings and some rare paintings hung on the walls. With our limited knowledge of art, we did not expect to see so many famous sculptures in the museum. Most religions allow statues. However, the Muslim faith is very strict about statues and sculptures. We did not know that sculpture was a prevalent visual art form and had equal importance to paintings in any western art museum.

Countless paintings covered all the walls of the rooms and spacious corridors. All the images were eye-catching and deserved to be adequately observed. Some of them were enormous. There were comfortable settees, here and there, where the art enthusiasts could sit down to study the paintings in detail.

Some of the collections are ancient and rare things. Murtuza bhai also said, 'I am not sure if anyone, other than the museum officials, knows the exact number of the Louvre's total collection. The museum is continuously acquiring new objects from all over the world. But unfortunately, the museum can display only a tiny portion of its total collection. The biggest museum in the world does not have adequate space to show more than thirty-five thousand artworks on a single day. However, the total collection is hundreds of thousands. For this reason, there is a saying that no one can see the total collection of the largest museum in the world.'

Murtuza bhai appreciated that we did not have an abundance of time and would not be able to have a thorough tour of the museum. He, therefore, made a selection of paintings and gave us the background information for those paintings. After a while, we asked him to show us the famous *Mona Lisa*. Murtuza bhai smiled and told us to be patient. He asked us to wait until the following day.

I found the environment in and around the Louvre so interesting. There was a festive atmosphere, crowded by truly international tourists of all ages. All with happy faces, showing expressions of excitement.

While listening to his commentary, I tried to relate to Murtuza bhai's description and the background information about the paintings. I realised that each image told us a unique story or documented a particular event or occasion. My new ability to interpret the meaning of the artist's work was exciting. The artworks suddenly became more interesting when I tried to see the inherent message the artist tried to give to the viewers. At the same time, each painting made us cast our minds on the artists' hard work. We thought it must have taken a few days to create these artworks. Murtuza bhai told us that some complicated paintings might take years to complete. 'You cannot imagine how much planning and thought go behind each brush stroke. There is another point you should know; to the artist, the work never finishes. He/she will always feel that there is room for improvement. For some artists, it is very difficult to finish the work; they believe that work hasn't been completed.'

We asked him, 'Don't the artists get bored working on the same project day after day?'

'On the contrary, they are often obsessed with their work. All artists think about their work all the time. It is challenging for them to decide that they have done everything possible.'

We eagerly waited to see the famous *Mona Lisa* on the second day. Before entering the room where the Mona Lisa was exhibited, we noticed a huge crowd. We had to struggle to get close to the painting. Uniformed stewards were busy pointing out to the visitors a sign on the wall warning them not to use flash when taking pictures. After seeing the Mona Lisa, our first impression was a huge disappointment. We had all seen photos of the Mona Lisa before, but we all believed the actual painting would be more attractive. Unfortunately, it did not meet our high expectations. Unlike the colourful, beautiful images all over the Louvre, the Mona Lisa looked like a very ordinary painting compared to the other huge images, which were so engaging that we couldn't stop looking at them. We could not find any reason why this modest-looking painting had become a priceless, precious object so famous that people worldwide came to see it.

Murtuza bhai was not surprised to see our disappointment. He had probably seen this reaction from other viewers he had given a guided tour. He explained, 'The Mona Lisa has become the most famous face in the world because the portrait was the first of a wave of paintings with an enigmatic expression. Before Leonardo da Vinci, no other artist had created a portrait that was so mysteriously attractive. From whichever position you look at the painting, you will feel she follows you with her seductive and fascinating smile. Leonardo da Vinci's extraordinary skill is known as the "Mona Lisa Effect".'

After Murtuza bhai's explanation, my eyes found new powers of observation. I looked at the painting with my new understanding to discover the inherent beauty of the face. Soon I realised that it wasn't her facial shape that made her smile; she expressed it through her eyes and seductive look. I studied the painting for some time and appreciated that her smile, surprisingly, penetrated my mind, as if she was telling me appealing stories. No wonder this painting caused such a sensation when it was once stolen from the museum. The whole museum was closed for two weeks to investigate the theft. After two years, when the Mona Lisa was recovered, the authorities took extra precautions to ensure it never got stolen again.

Murtuza bhai explained, 'The Mona Lisa is not the only famous painting in the Louvre. 'Liberty Leading the people (a painting by Delacroix about the French Revolution) and the 'Raft of the Medusa' (by Géricault) found a place in the Louvre. In addition to the famous paintings and sculptures, the Louvre is always a pleasant surprise to visitors. If you can manage to come back, try to see Napoleon's lavish dining room, with its elegant furniture and exquisite painting overhead.'

Murtuza bhai finally said, 'It is not only the Louvre, you will find the whole of Paris is like a fascinating museum. You will be amazed when you see the Notre Dame, a medieval Catholic cathedral. This cathedral is one of a kind for its sculptural decoration. I wish you had come to Paris in the summertime, when the whole city looks like it's going through a joyous festival. Even in this cold winter, if you walk from here to the Arc de Triomphe through the Tuileries Garden and by the famous Avenue des Champs-Elysees, you will feel you are passing through a different world.'

Sightseeing in Paris with Murtuza bhai

We learned that this city has had different nicknames at different times. The most popular nicknames for Paris are

'La Ville Lumière', the city of light, the 'City of Love, and 'The city of romance. The other nicknames given to Paris are City of Art and City of Fashions.

Although Paris was the third city in the world to introduce gas street lighting (after London in 1807 and Baltimore in 1816), Paris is known as the 'city of light' because Paris's street lighting is on such a grand scale, not lighting just one street as in London. Besides, thirty-three of its thirty-seven bridges is illuminated at night. Paris, therefore, is a dazzling city like no other.

Sightseeing in Paris

Many people also feel that Paris earned this title not just for illuminating the whole city, literally, but most importantly because Paris is considered to have enlightened the field of entertainment. Paris's arts and culture have always been a source of envy for many countries. Famous theatres, clubs and music halls have kept them fascinated. The Moulin Rouge, for example, is probably best known as the birthplace of the famous dance known as the 'Can-Can'. Besides the Moulin Rouge, other famous venues include the Lido de Paris, Crazy Horse, and Nouvelle Eve. Tourists will never feel they have not thoroughly fulfilled their expectations.

Most visitors find Paris the most romantic city in the

world. One can find romantic vibes in Paris like no other. Everything, including the architecture throughout the city, is dedicated to love. We could understand why Paris was called the City of Love. The monuments, sculptures, gardens, and even the beautiful colourful buildings in the residential neighbourhoods, combine to mesmerise the viewer. Most visitors are captivated by the wonders all around them. There is a famous wall known as the Wall of Love in the Montmartre district. The wall is covered by the phrase 'I love you in almost every language on earth'. I am not aware of any other country where a wall or a place has been dedicated for the visitors to express the famous phrase, 'I love you, in a public place.

Talking about the Montmartre district, I have to mention the famous artists' village on the hilltop. From 1880 until the First World War, France enjoyed economic prosperity and a period of cultural innovation. France, particularly Paris, saw remarkable advancements in the cultural and artistic spheres. In Montmartre, the arts flourished, and artists came from all over France and beyond. Montmartre became known as the artists' village. Many famous artists lived there, including Monet, Renoir and Van Gough. The world-famous painter, Picasso, born in the neighbouring country, Spain, moved to Paris's artist village when he was nineteen and became the most famous painter of the modern age. I remembered the legendary Indian singer, Tansen, who was born outside Uttar Pradesh but became one of the most celebrated singers of all time in India after he moved to Lucknow. This place was always in favour of advancing the arts and culture in India.

Therefore, it seems a universal theme that a particular area attracts a specific group of geniuses to develop and expose their talents.

Murtuza bhai was right. We found everything pleasing and remarkable wherever we went and whichever way we turned. It was a feast for our eyes. One can see exquisitely compelling sculptures made of bronze, copper and bright white marvel everywhere. They were life-size, in different colours, dark, green and white, and placed not only in the gardens and squares but on the bridges, riverside roads and in many places where one could not imagine seeing an attractive sculpture.

It was not only the pleasant sights all around Paris, but to a great extent, the sounds too, which made visitors fall in love with Paris. A non-French-speaking person who does not understand a word in French will be entranced by the sound of the language. Even when two French people have a fierce argument, a foreigner feels as if they are reciting a sweet poem. Perhaps that is why so many people think that French is the most romantic language in the world.

We devoted most of our first few days in Paris to visit the Louvre. However, we also wanted to visit The Eiffel Tower, Arc de Triomphe, and walk on the most famous street in Paris, Champs-Élysées. Like the Eiffel Tower, the Arc de Triomphe is another imposing structure in Paris and another landmark of France.

When we saw the India gate in New Delhi, we wondered why the India Gate looked like the Arc de Triomphe in Paris. We then found out that Edwin Lutyens was inspired to design the India Gate in New Delhi by the design of the Arc de

Triomphe. Each time we visited the Eiffel Tower, we felt like going straight back there again. Until we saw this massive tower with our own eyes, we had not realised how tall it was. In 1889, when the Eiffel Tower was constructed, it was the tallest tower in the world and retained that record for over forty years.

The Eiffel Tower was originally constructed as part of the 1889 World Fair. The tower was designed as the entrance to the event. The whole world was impressed by the daring design and the sheer scale of the structure. In addition, this tower made a bold statement about France's engineering know-how. People who came to attend the world fair were so amazed at the tower that the other objects in the fair that they came to see became secondary.

Sight-seeing in Paris

At the World Fair, one attendee, Sir John Bickerstaffe, Mayor of Blackpool, was so impressed by the Eiffel Tower that he decided to build a similar tower on the English seafront, the Blackpool Tower, in 1891. As time has gone by, more and more countries have built replicas of the Eiffel Tower. I understand that more than eighty countries have constructed imitations of this iconic tower.

BOAT RIDE

The river Seine starts in the northeast of France and flows like an elegant lady to meet the English Channel. Like most other rivers, the route of this river is not exactly a straight line. Instead, it veers from left to right and vice versa, like a dance move by a gracious lady. On the way, the Seine passes through the heart of Paris, adding a unique charm to the city. Many of the bridges across the Seine work like the ornaments of the city, as they are so attractive due to their sculptural construction. Fascinating to the onlookers are the famous Pont Alexandre III with Art Nouveau lamps and the Pont Neuf, the oldest bridge on the river Seine. In the evening, light emitting from these bridges and the buildings on both banks reflects on the water, giving the Seine a tranquil atmosphere.

One embassy staff member told us that there were boats offering sightseeing tours on the Seine, and we would not regret it if we went on this boat cruise.

The day before we left Paris, we paid yet another visit to the Eiffel Tower and then got on to one of the cruise boats. We thanked the officer in the Bangladesh embassy for suggesting we go on a boat cruise. We were amazed to see all the famous buildings and fascinating bridges, which we would have missed had we not been on this cruise.

We thoroughly enjoyed our hour-long cruise, which took us past the Louvre and the Champs-Elysées and then back to the Eiffel Tower in the early evening, when Paris started glowing golden in the sunset. The unique atmosphere created by the sunset does not last long. For this reason, everybody takes a short break to enjoy the special moment. On the river Seine, however, the sunset effect seems to last for longer. Before the natural light went to sleep, artificial light emitted from other cruise boats, floating restaurants, bridges, and above all, from all the buildings on both banks sustained and maintained sunset effects longer. These lights reflecting on the river created a fascinating view. Natural golden sunset and artificial light blended so nicely that they made a breathtaking scene. The atmosphere was so calm and peaceful! I could only feel it in my heart; no way could I express my feelings in words. I wished the world could stop at that moment. However, I was aware that the boat was moving, and this journey was coming to an end very soon. From afar, we saw the Eiffel Tower glowing in the evening light, and we felt that the tower was waiting to greet us. We thoroughly enjoyed the boat journey and thought it was worth every cent.

Paris is elegant and glamorous. It exerts such a strong romantic appeal that it is difficult not to feel it. Pleasant sights in all directions attract everybody, no matter how hard their hearts are. The mixture of beautiful architectural splendour is visible everywhere. The iconic Eiffel Tower looked like the jewel in the crown, and the river Seine adorned the city with its smooth flowing through the city's heart, making the whole town a piece of artwork. One cannot help but strongly feel that everything seems to be blossoming and emitting a sensational air of romance.

We wished it was summertime and we could have stayed much longer in Paris, but we had to leave and make our way to Calais, a ferry port in northern France. We reached Calais on 16 October 1972, stayed overnight in a hotel and the following day, 17 October 1972, we got into a hovercraft sailing towards Dover, England.

It was our first journey on a hovercraft. We had heard of this vehicle before. We were puzzled when we learned it was amphibious; it could travel both on land and water.

We then understood that a hovercraft is a vehicle that glides over a smooth surface on a cushion of air. In those days, the hovercraft making the crossing could carry over two hundred and fifty passengers and up to thirty cars.

Because it is no longer commercially viable, the hovercraft has become history. However, there is still one commercial hovercraft service left; it operates a regular timetable, taking passengers between Portsmouth and the Isle of Wight.

TWENTY-SIX

London

Stepping on British soil for the first time, we were excited, feeling that there would no longer be any language problems and that we could ride our bikes on the left-hand side of the road! But my real excitement was much deeper than the apparent advantages. Ever since I was a teen, I had dreamt of visiting two cities. One was Kolkata, and the other was London. These were not just my dreams. These were my earnest desires. My fascination for these two cities did not slowly disappear or weaken as I grew but remained as strong as ever.

Visiting Kolkata was a dream comes true, and then, I eagerly looked forward to my other desire, to see London. Having toured India and some European countries, I was content to have increased my knowledge of the old civilisation. Britain is undoubtedly the pioneer of the advancement of modern society, and I hoped that Britain will boost my understanding of contemporary civilisation.

Born in a commonwealth country, we all had considerable knowledge of Britain's past and present. I had already made a mental list of must-see spots in London. The Soap Box at Speaker's Corner in Hyde Park was one place that drew our attention, as it symbolised the freedom of speech. I knew that Karl Marx, Lenin, George Orwell, and many other famous people were regular orators on the Hyde Park speaker's corner. I felt it was a great idea and an opportunity for people to stand up and speak about anything freely on any Sunday morning at Hyde Park corner.

Besides Hyde Park Corner, Trafalgar Square, Piccadilly Circus, the famous Oxford Street, the Mall leading to Buckingham Palace, and many other places were on my list. And I had a longstanding wish to visit Madame Tussauds after reading a newspaper article about this wonder. So I promised myself that when I visited London, the first place I would like to see would be Madame Tussauds.

Since starting college, I have often visited the British Council, which was very close to my home in Dhaka. I used to go there to use its library, meet friends and occasionally watch free black-and-white English movies. I always had an excellent, enjoyable time there. I particularly enjoyed turning the pages of prominent British newspapers printed on fragile materials like tissue paper. Later I learnt that the newspapers were sent from the UK by air, so they had to be very light in weight. I remember reading an article in one of the British broadsheet papers praising my favourite all-rounder cricketer, Asif Iqbal, when he showed off his formidable batting at Lord's. The reporter stated, 'Until we witnessed Asif's brilliant batting, we did not know how beautiful this game was!' The mother of all cricket grounds, Lord's, has always been on my wish list of must-see places in London.

After visiting quite a few countries, I realised that most countries have a fascinating past, but I did not know much about them until I had been there. Similarly, although I knew a lot of things about London, I correctly guessed that there would be many exciting points of interest in London that I didn't know about or hadn't even heard of.

We know the UK's long history of inventions and innovations. We read a lot about Industrial Revolution. However, I was unaware of the Agricultural Revolution until much later; this also started in Britain shortly before the Industrial Revolution. Although the first agricultural revolution occurred in the Middle East in prehistoric times, it was in Britain that the modern-day Agricultural Revolution occurred in the 16th century.

The Industrial Revolution changed the mode of manufacturing goods forever, moving away from home to large factories. Also, in the wake of the Industrial Revolution, many further technological innovations originated in Britain. Other inventions in Britain flashed back while we were pedalling on the left-hand side of the road.

Soon after we left the port area in Dover, we realised that we did not have any drinking water. Noticing a house near the main road, we stopped and knocked on the door. A young boy came out and was surprised to see three foreigners on their bikes! He was interested in the 'World Tourist Bangladesh' sign on the leather baskets at the back of our bikes. He said something to us with obvious enthusiasm. We could hardly understand what he said. We asked the boy if he could give us some water to drink. We noticed that he was struggling to understand us. I took a pen and wrote down 'Drinking Water' to save confusion and time. The boy smiled and said, 'Oh. Wo'o ta?' His mother came to the door, hearing the noise. The boy excitedly explained to his mum about us and that we wanted to have some drinking water.

So much for our good feelings about our expectation that we would have no language problem in the UK!

I remembered that Matin Bhai explained to us earlier, in Geneva, that because of the striking difference between our accent and the local English, we would find it difficult to understand them and vice versa. Long afterwards, we learnt that the local English people do not pronounce the letter 'R' if it is the last letter in the word. Also, occasionally, the letter 'T' becomes silent, or it is pronounced differently if it is in the middle of a word.

Since our arrival in the UK, we had hardly seen the sun. It was struggling to come out with a smile to say hello to us. Thick fog guarded the sun and did not allow it even to take a quick peek at us. As it was wintertime, it got darker much sooner than we expected. We did not feel safe riding in these conditions and began to look for a place for the night.

We left the main road and entered a village to find a place to stay. We had become quite used to knocking on the doors of people who were strangers to us. A gentleman came out in response to the doorbell. He apologised for not having enough room to put us up for the night. He was kind enough to point out the church, not far from his house, and suggested we approach the priest there.

The priest welcomed us and said, 'It would be my pleasure to arrange your stay for the night at my house.' He led us to his residence, which was inside the church compound.

His wife and daughter were pleased to have three strange guests in their house. After we settled down, we explained the purpose of our tour and gave them a description of our experiences in different countries. After dinner, we found a nice cosy sleeping place made ready for us. But the most welcoming experience for us was the hot water bottles inside our blankets! In Bangladesh, we never used a hot water bottle to stay warm in bed. Instead, we usually switched the ceiling fan on to cool us down for a sound sleep. In the cold winter in the UK, the hot water bottles under the quilts felt like a gift from heaven!

In the morning, I telephoned my uncle, who lived in North London. My uncle was pleased to hear that we were in the UK, but he was a bit concerned that we would get lost and not be able to find his place. He gave me a long talk, explaining that it would be impossible for us to cycle from Kent to North London. I convinced him, saying that we had not got lost on our long journey from Bangladesh to Kent, so we would surely be able to find our way to his house in London. Nonetheless, he gave me a long list of landmarks, like ‘Kings Cross’, ‘Finsbury Park’ etc.

My uncle was right. It seemed extremely difficult to plan our route because we needed an A-Z. It was too difficult to ask people for directions before we made every turn. When we reached Greenwich, We telephoned my uncle and gave him our location. He insisted that we take a train to Finsbury Park. He warned us there was no direct service from Greenwich to Finsbury Park and explained how to change trains.

We did not have to think about it for long; we just took the next train and headed to Finsbury Park. We mostly travelled underground, so we did not know that the weather was worsening rapidly. When we emerged from the Underground, we saw dense fog enveloping the city, and visibility had dropped to almost zero. The thick fog seemed to have become tangible; it was as if we could push the moisture out of our way with our hands to see where we were heading. The yellow street lamps seemed too weak to hold back the solid grey mass. I felt the lampposts worked like a lighthouse, giving the lost sailors a sense of direction but not illuminating the surroundings. Besides the poor visibility, the cold penetrated us all the way to our bones.

My uncle had given us really detailed directions to his house from the station. We did not want to bother him to come to the station to fetch us. But because of the thick fog, we could not read the street signs to find the road names. So, we asked a few people for directions.

We realised that if we had not taken the train from Greenwich, it would have been quite late when we reached my uncle's house.

Both my uncle and aunty knew Khokan, as he was my maternal cousin. I introduced Babul to them. They welcomed Babul warmly and helped him to feel at home.

Before I left Bangladesh, I had heard the exciting news that Deepa, our new cousin, had arrived. I couldn't wait to see my new cousin and went to meet her. She was just over two months old and was lying in her cot, wide awake; probably, she heard the loud voices in the house. Deepa welcomed me with a smile. However, my meeting with Deepa was very brief as everybody was ready to start having dinner, and aunty was calling me to join them.

While we enjoyed a delicious dinner, we did what we had been doing for the last few months whenever we met someone for the first time. That is, we talked about our experiences on tour. My aunt told us they had a small group of close friends who visited each other's houses almost every weekend for dinner and gossip. She asked us to keep ourselves free on Friday, as they had an invitation for dinner. Their host, Mirza chacha (uncle), would be delighted to meet us.

The following day, we visited the Bangladesh High Commission. His Excellency Abdus Sultan, the Bangladesh High Commissioner in London, greeted us warmly. Hearing that we had reached London the previous night, the first thing he inquired about was our accommodation. When he heard that we did not have a proper place to stay, he immediately telephoned someone to arrange accommodation for us at the Bangladesh Bhavan, a student hostel on Highbury Hill in north London. Next, he gave us a brief background history of the hostel. Originally known as East Pakistan House, it was a student hostel for students from East Pakistan. However, as soon as Bangladesh became independent, the hostel's name changed to 'Bangladesh Bhavan', but it remained a hostel for Bangladeshi students

BANGLADESH TODAY 6 LONDON, NOVEMBER 1, 1972

Three Bangladesh cyclists who have been touring the world arrived in London recently. They called on the High Commissioner of Bangladesh Syed Abdus Sultan and are seen with him in front of the High Commission building. The cyclists are (from right) Jamaluddin Md. Hassan, Anwar Uddin Ahmed, and Mahmud Abdul Quayyum.

Bangladesh Cyclists in London

Three students of Dacca University who are on a world tour by bicycle "to convey the heartiest message of goodwill and goodwishes of the people of Bangladesh to the people of various countries of the world" have arrived London on October 18.

The cyclists, Mr. Jamal Uddin (23), Mr. Anwaruddin Ahmed (20) and Mr. Mahmud Abdul Quayum (24), who were members of Mukti Bahini during liberation struggle, left Dacca on April 7 and meanwhile visited India, Greece, Yugoslavia, Italy, Switzerland, West Germany Belgium, France. After touring Great Britain they hope to visit USA, Canada, Japan, Philippines, Indonesia, Thailand and Burma before returning to Bangladesh sometime in 1973.

During their tour of countries they met dignitaries of various countries including the Prime Minister of India, Mrs. Indira Gandhi and presented them the national flag of Bangladesh.

Bangladesh Cyclists in London is a reproduction of a news article in Bangladesh Today published on 1 November 1972 by Bangladesh High Commission, London.

With His Excellency Abdus Sultan, the Bangladesh High Commissioner in London

After arranging our accommodation, His Excellency asked us to tell him about our tour. He wanted to hear about the exciting parts and the most challenging experiences. He was pleased to hear that we were well received by the governments and the people of all the countries we had visited. We told him that we were surprised to find that people of all ages were well aware of our liberation struggle. The High Commissioner then wanted to know about our plans, how long we expected to stay in London, our next destination etc. We explained that we had decided to take a long pause from our tour and pass the winter in the UK. Then, in the spring, we would proceed towards the USA and return to Bangladesh after visiting Japan and other countries. Hearing our plans, The High Commissioner appeared to be lost in his thoughts. After a while, he asked us to come and see him on Monday afternoon.

We went to the Bangladesh Bhavan from the High Commission Office. The warden told us that, luckily, three rooms were vacant. He told us that our rooms would be ready by the next day. We were happy to have our room after a long time. On the road, we always shared a room with teammates. My uncle and aunt insisted we stay with them for a few more days. She said it would be challenging to cook our dinner in the hostel. She reminded us about our invitation to Mirza Chacha's house the following Friday. My uncle suggested that we move to the hostel on Sunday.

One day my aunty told us that if we always travelled by underground train, we would not see very much of London. She said, 'However, if you travel by bus you will not only be able to see London better, but also it will be cheaper.' Aunty added that we could also ride on the open-top tourist bus, which would pass all the most famous tourist attractions in London. Taking their advice, we started travelling by bus when we were not in a hurry. One day we got on a tourist bus, and it was really exciting. We saw so many interesting places. We would not have had the opportunity to see some of those sights if we had not opted to take the bus. We made a note of some attractions to revisit at a later date.

On Friday, we continued sightseeing until it was getting dark. The scene in the evening was quite spectacular. However, we cut short our roaming when we remembered the instruction to get back home by 5.30 pm to attend the invitation.

Mirza chacha's place was not far from my uncle's house, just a short drive. When we reached his place, many guests had already arrived. I was surprised to see them most informal, although they were friends rather than relations. I painfully remembered how Bangladeshi culture was beginning to compromise itself by copying Western culture. Under this influence, traditional Bengali culture was fading away in Bangladesh. People were becoming individualistic and having formal relationships with others. Therefore, I was pleasantly surprised to see the Bangladeshis in London retained this sweet aspect of the Bangladeshi culture, although they were far away from home. The guests' behaviour took me back to my childhood times.

As soon as we entered Mirza chacha's house, some people yelled my name. They had never seen me, Babul or

Khokan and did not know which one of us was Jamal. There were some teenagers among the guests. They approached and asked me, 'Jamal bhai, is it true that you came from Bangladesh by bicycle?' We felt everybody at the party accepted us as one of them instantly.

One scene provoked my memories of old Bangladeshi culture; I saw one uncle enter the kitchen, take off the lids of some of the dishes and, in a happy voice, say, 'These look delicious!' I couldn't imagine a non-related adult male entering a woman's kitchen and inspecting the dishes unless they had an informal relationship. Unfortunately, my uncle and aunt and some of their friends whom I met nearly fifty years ago at that party in Mirza chacha's house have passed away. However, my relationship with their family members continues to date, as if we are blood-related.

On Monday, we went to the High Commission office and found that the High Commissioner was with some people. He invited us in and told us he had invited a few Bangladeshi businessmen and prominent community leaders to meet us. After he introduced us to his guests, he told them that we would be staying in London for a few months to pass the winter and would need their help and support during our stay.

The community leaders were only too pleased to help us. Everybody got engaged in a discussion with us about our tour. They gave us their contact details and an invitation to approach them for any help we needed. One of the community leaders was Mrs Baksh, chair of the 'Bangladesh Mahila Samiti' (women's group). She told us that she would drop into the hostel to see us soon.

One day, the Bangladesh High Commission Office informed us that we had an invitation from a charismatic Labour politician, John Stonehouse, MP. We had heard of John Stonehouse before. He was a cabinet minister in Harold Wilson's Government. He actively supported the Bangladesh independence movement and raised funds for our liberation war. He was a famous person in the Bangladeshi community in London. Mr Stonehouse praised us for undertaking this goodwill tour and wished us the best for the rest of the tour.

Since 23 March 1971, when I left Dhaka, and until I arrived in the UK in October 1972, I was a refugee, a freedom fighter and finally had been on the move as a world cycle tourist. For these reasons, I was unaware of what was happening worldwide during our liberation war. Only after I came to the UK did I start catching up with the news in the last year and seven months.

I was overwhelmed hearing the news that people, particularly the Bangladeshi community in London, were so concerned about what was happening in Bangladesh that they generously donated to help the freedom fighter to win the war. I was moved to hear stories that some people donated the whole of their weekly wages. However, one of the exciting pieces of information that thrilled me most was that the Bangladesh liberation war raised the level of international political solidarity to a new phenomenon. Besides typical demonstrations and rallies condemning the brutal Pakistani army dictators, the world-famous Beatle star George Harrison and equally world-famous sitarist Ravi Shankar organised a concert for Bangladesh. The purpose of the concert was twofold.

Firstly, to raise money for the Bangladeshi refugee and, secondly and most importantly, to form a world opinion against the genocide caused by the brutal Pakistani army dictators. This concert was the first of its kind, now popularly known as a benefit concert. About 14 years later, Sir Bob Geldof organised the second benefit concert, the famous 'Live Aid', for the famine victims in Ethiopia. Nowadays, benefit concerts have become a popular form of raising awareness and, at the same time, raising funds for good causes.

The children of Villa Theressa School in Mumbai gave us the idea of how people worldwide showed solidarity towards the cause of our liberation war.

When the freedom fighters were engaged in the guerilla war against the Pakistan army, sympathetic artists raised money for us in Madison Sq. Garden in New York. People from all walks of life wished for our victory. For this reason, we did not fight and win the war alone, but the war was fought by all freedom lovers worldwide.

Besides my uncle and aunt, I had some close childhood friends who were settled in the UK. One childhood friend, Azam, did not wait for me to visit him; he came to see me as soon as he heard the news that I was in London. Azam gave me the contact details of all my other friends and acquaintances in London.

My childhood mentor, Lutfur Rahman Shahjahan, was delighted to hear the news of my arrival. Shahjahan bhai had come to London to study law. His younger brother, Sohrab, was my closest friend.

Sohrab (Dr Atiq Rahman) is now a world-renowned

environmentalist. He was a co-recipient of the 2007 Nobel Peace Prize and lead author of the Intergovernmental Panel on Climate Change (IPCC) Fourth Assessment. He also won the 'Champions of the Earth Award' for the Asia Pacific region in 2008. Sohrab would always keep us informed of Shahjahan Bhai. One day, he told me that Shahjahn bhai had married in the UK to the only daughter of Jobeda Khanom, a famous academic in Bangladesh.

Back home in Dhaka, Shahjahan bhai was one of the founder members of our sports/cultural club, 'Jubo Sangsad' (Youth Organisation), and he was a popular person in our neighbourhood for his community and social work. So we all went to see Sahjahan bhai hearing the news of his arrival in Bangladesh. Shahjahan bhai always kept us interested with his inspirational talks. He would tell us a lot about the exciting aspects of London life.

What a surprise it was when Shahjahan bhai introduced his exceptionally charming wife. None of us knew that his wife, Munni bhabi, would accompany him. We were pleased to find Munni Bhabi very affectionate as if she had known us for a long time. She gave us lots of presents, sweets and particularly foreign cigarettes, which were very expensive in Bangladesh. As neither Sohrab nor I smoked, all our friends started pleading with us to give them our share of the cigarettes in exchange for their chocolates!

When I telephoned Shahjahan bhai, Munni bhabi answered my call. I introduced myself. I thought she would struggle to work out who I was. But although it had been so many years since I met her in Bangladesh, and only for a short time, she remembered me as soon as I mentioned that I was Sohrab's friend. She cordially invited me to visit them soon.

Shahjahan Bhai, Munni Bhabi and their only daughter, Tanya, who was just over a year old, lived in Russell Square. Both Shahjahan bhai and Munni bhabi were active in community work. Shahjahan Bhai was a lawyer by profession. He was also a part-time teacher. However, his hobby as a community activist appeared to be his most important job. Munni bhabi also was a well-known socialite in the Bangladeshi community in London. She was a cultural events organiser and community activist. She played an essential role during the Bangladesh Independence movement. A few years after we came to the UK, Shajahan bhai and Munni bhabi took the initiative to found the Bangladesh Centre at 24 Pembridge Gardens, which housed the first Bangladesh High Commission in the UK. For this reason, 24 Pembridge Gardens has a great emotional attachment for many Bangladeshis. Shahjahan bhai and Munni bhabi successfully formed a trust and bought the property for the Bangladesh Centre.

I was dying to meet Shahjahan bhai and Munni bhabi again. I was also keen to see Shahjahan bhai and Sohrab's sister, Baby. She was settled in the UK with her husband, Sahadat Hossain, and lived in Camden Town, not far from Shahjahan bhai's house. However, I could not find the time to meet them immediately because of other essential engagements.

Finally, after a few days, I found the time to visit them.

When I entered Shajahan bhai's house, I felt like I was in a community centre. There was a constant stream of people coming and going. People would drop in any time at the weekends, and later I learned that some would come in the weekday evening as well. The house seemed to be a meeting place for many people.

When I arrived, there were already a few people there. While some left, some others came in. Azam told me that often some of the visitors would stay overnight in the spare room and on the settee in the living room. Later I discovered that when too many people stayed overnight, some had to resort to the floor to pass the night. Shahjahan bhai's younger brother, and my closest friend, Sohrab, came to the UK to do his PhD at Brunel University. He would often visit them at the weekend. Another childhood friend, Thandu, would occasionally come from South Shields, where he studied marine engineering. Thandu often would stay for the weekend. As Sohrab, Thandu and I were younger than the other guests, we had to give up desirable places to the senior guests. I remember, once Sohrab and I had to make our beds in the corridor! At that time, I didn't know that one day I would move into Shajahan bhai and Munni bhabi's place to live with them.

The makeup of the crowd who would meet almost every weekend was intriguing. Most of the regular visitors came from a left-wing political persuasion, and a few were affiliated with other liberal and progressive political parties. I remember some people from the Awami League party, the ruling party of Bangladesh, were regular guests. One was the former press secretary of Bangabandhu, Sheikh Mujibur Rahman. The discussion often turned into a fascinating debate. Besides Shajahan bhai, one more person was a lawyer, but most were teachers and civil servants. There would be non-political discussions as well. Sometimes there would be a singing session as some people would perform to entertain the whole group. Sometimes a small group would settle on the floor to play bridge, and sometimes just two people would find a corner to start playing chess. I discovered that the reasons for so many people visiting Shahjahan bhai's place were manifold. Firstly it was to have an excellent time, gossiping with like-minded people. However, I felt that one of the key reasons was to enjoy Munni bhabi's delicious food.

Workaholic Munni bhabi would get up early and go out to get newspapers and other shopping for breakfast while we were still asleep. She would then get one or two volunteers to give her a hand in preparing a late breakfast for everybody.

Although we did not have to pay for our accommodation at the Bangladesh Bhavan, and the hostel was conveniently close to the Underground station, we never fell in love with the place. Firstly, the building was extremely cold, and secondly, there was a lack of facilities for interaction with each other. While it was an ideal place for students, we felt we would be better off finding alternative accommodation. Babul and Khokan contacted two community leaders we had met at the High Commission office earlier. Khokan and Babul found jobs and housing with two community leaders, Khokan in Central London and Babul in South London. My uncle and aunt suggested I move back to their place, as the hostel was unsuitable.

Having stayed together for nearly seven months, I missed my teammates' company. However, we were always in touch and often met at Shahjahan bhai and Shahadat bhai's houses. These places seemed to have become our second home. Baby's husband, Shahadat bhai, was a very humorous person. He would keep us amused with his witty jokes. Two of Bangladesh's most popular and celebrated film actors visited Baby's house. One was Anwar Hossain, and the other one was Subash Dutta. Subash Datta was popularly known as a humorous person. However, he stopped telling us jokes when he realised that Sahadat bhai's delivery of jokes was much more enjoyable than his. He said, 'I cannot match the master. I give up!'

Unlike in Shajahan bhai's house, in Shadat bhai's and Baby's house, the gathering was non-political and purely social.

One day the High Commission office informed us that Shaymal Lodh, from the Bengali department of the BBC, wanted to interview us. Like Mark Tully, the BBC bureau chief in India, Mr Shaymal Lodh was popular amongst Bengali-speaking people worldwide.

Mr Lodh suggested to us that we meet him in Trafalgar Square. He asked us to bring our cycles.

Khokan, Babul, and I met at Bangladesh Bhavan to get our bikes as we left them in the hostel's basement.

We had been to Trafalgar square a few times by bus, and the route was familiar. However, it had been some time since we last rode our cycles. So it was good fun to be on the bikes again.

Trafalgar Square, in central London, is one of the most famous public squares in the UK. It has long been a landmark of London. After Lord Nelson won the Battle of Trafalgar, this square was built to memorialise his victory. However, I did not know the Battle's details and the whereabouts of the place. Later I learnt that the Battle took place off the coast of Spain, near Cape Trafalgar.

A giant statue of Lord Nelson, the victorious admiral, stands in the centre of the square.

Trafalgar Square became a centre of national democracy. Protest marches end at the square for rallies and public meetings. Before the New Year celebrations moved to the London Eye, they would always be celebrated in this square.

In the past, the image of Trafalgar Square was closely associated with pigeons. One of the fascinating tourist activities in the square was feeding the friendly birds. However, because it was too much for the authorities to clean the pigeon droppings, the Mayor of London banned tourists from feeding pigeons in Trafalgar Square in 2003. As a result, no one can see pigeons in Trafalgar Square anymore.

The National Gallery, on the edge of the square, adds to the historical beauty of this area. This gallery is home to a highly significant collection of paintings from from European art history. Van Gogh's *Sunflowers*, and *The Entombment*, by Michelangelo are among many valuable and delightful artworks that have found their place in this gallery. The gallery houses a collection of over 2,300 paintings dating from the mid-13th century to the beginning of the twentieth. It has always been a must-visit place in London.

Although we knew Mr Lodh by name, we had never met him. However, finding each other on a crowded afternoon in Trafalgar Square was not difficult. Long-haired Mr Lodh was holding a BBC microphone, accompanied by a cameraman, and we also stood out in the crowd, with our cycles and in uniform. The tourists became curious and took a break from feeding the pigeons to watch us. After the photo sessions and a brief discussion, Mr Lodh told us he would be interested in interviewing us again, this time in the BBC studio at Bush House.

On returning to Bangladesh Bhavan from Trafalgar Square, I noticed we were passing through a road full of bookshops. I hadn't seen many bookshops when we passed this road going in the other direction. Out of curiosity, I looked for the name of the road and was thrilled to find it was Charing Cross Road! Immediately I remembered the short story – *84 Charing Cross Road* – which appeared in the Readers Digest a few years earlier. I remembered how much I enjoyed the captivating story. Everybody who used to subscribe to the most popular monthly Readers Digest magazine was moved by this touching short story, narrated through a series of letters between an author in the USA, Helene Hanff, and Mr Frank Percy Doel, a bookseller in London. Frank Percy Doel worked at the bookshop Marks & Co at 84 Charing Cross Road. The short story became so popular worldwide that later it was published as a book and became an instant bestseller. I bumped into the *84 Charing*

Cross Road film version a few years ago. Unfortunately, I felt the film was less appealing than the written version.

After seeing the 84 Charing Cross Road shop, I looked for Foyles, a famous bookshop. I had heard so much about it from people who had been to London. For a long time, Foyles was regarded as the largest bookshop in the world. It was on the same road, not far from 84 Charing Cross Road.

A few weeks passed, and London's foggy outlook did not improve much. London continued to disappoint us. On my first meeting with Shahjahan bhai, I expressed my disappointment and told Shajahan bhai, 'So this is London? What a disappointment!'

Shahjahan bhai smiled and replied, 'Well, London is not dazzling like Paris or highly developed like Germany. So understandably, it is more difficult to appreciate the apparent beauty of London. However, if you can discover the inherent beauty of this city, you will never find a second city as attractive as London.'

As days passed, I began to discover the inherent beauty of this city. Extraordinary rarities started to reveal themselves. Incredible and unexpected wonders began to emerge. When I heard about the NHS (National Health Service) and learned more about the welfare state, I thought that the UK was the ideal country for almost anybody.

One day I was taken aback when I read in the newspaper about a traffic warden sticking a parking ticket on Prime Minister Edward Heath's car because it was parked on a yellow line. The driver came running to inform the traffic warden that it was the Prime Minister's car. While sticking the ticket on the windscreen, the traffic warden replied, 'Ask the Prime Minister to change the law, and then I will not give him a ticket.' I wondered if a traffic warden could even go near the Prime Minister or the president's car in any other country. It was not only the atmosphere of doing the right thing fearlessly but also asserting one's rights, which was rare in other countries.

While I was at college, I heard about the soap box in Hyde Park. Visiting Hyde Park was on my list of must-see things in London. My aunty suggested that I get off the bus at the Tottenham Court Road stop and walk on Oxford Street towards Marble Arch to see Oxford Street, one of the most famous shopping streets in the world. My aunty also suggested that on my return journey, I turn right into Regent Street, another famous shopping street in London. At the end of Regent Street, I could see Piccadilly Circus. I had heard of Oxford Street and Piccadilly Circus before I came to this country, and these were also on my list of must-see places in London.

Oxford Street

I had a thrilling experience walking on Oxford Street, towards Marble Arch. I did not wish to buy anything, nor did I feel I could afford to shop on such a posh shopping street. However, window shopping turned out to be good fun. I had a moment of confusion when I noticed Bond Street Underground on my left. The name Bond Street seemed so familiar to me. I struggled for some time with why and how I had heard the title of this street. I had heard of Oxford Street because of the amazing shops, but I couldn't put my finger on how I had heard of Bond Street. After a while, I gave up and started walking towards Marble Arch, but the name Bond Street played like a broken record in my head. Suddenly I remembered the name Old Kent Road! And then the words of Pall Mall, Mayfair, Park Lane and many London streets and places flooded my memory. I then realised that I knew the names of these Roads from the Monopoly board game!

As soon as I thought of Monopoly, I couldn't help but start reminiscing about the past. So my thought returned to the 1960s when my friend Azam's brother-in-law brought a game of Monopoly from England. It was exciting when Azam broke the news of this new board game, utterly unknown to most of us. At that time, none of us was conversant with English, and we needed help and guidance from our elders to learn how to play this most fascinating and engaging game. So whenever we could not play outdoor sports, we would settle down for a long session with the fascinating indoor game of Monopoly. I fondly remember our enjoyable time playing Monopoly in Azam's place on most rainy days.

After coming to the UK, I learned that besides being a popular shopping street, Oxford Street was also famous for its Christmas lights. Every year a celebrity turns on the attractive Christmas lights, and about a million people visit Oxford Street to enjoy the sight.

Just before I came to the end of Oxford Street, I noticed a huge green open space emerging. I realised that it was part of Hyde Park.

Hyde Park Corner

Hyde Park was famous as the location of Speakers' Corner, where self-appointed orators could stand up and talk about anything they had strong feelings about. Famous people, like Karl Marx, Vladimir Lenin and George Orwell, often used to speak there to demonstrate free speech. Since it started in Hyde Park in 1866, the concept of a speaker's corner was established in other parks in the UK and later in other countries. Freedom of speech was indeed a step forward to a better civilisation.

Britain's inherent beauty was unfolding in front of my eyes as the days went by.

On my way back, I took a bus to Trafalgar Square via Regents Street. However, unlike Oxford Street, the standard of business in Regents Street was impossibly high. I realised that this street exclusively catered for wealthy and upper-class people. Therefore, I took the proper decision of window shopping on this famous street by bus and not by walking as I did on Oxford Street.

One of the most famous shops in the world, Harrods, is in Kensington, in West London. At one time, Harrods was one of the biggest shops in the world. Nowadays, one can see a few other big shops in South Korea, the USA and other places. However, Harrods is still far and away the most famous shop in the world. Harrods offers a selection of the most luxurious and expensive goods.

Piccadilly Circus

Anthony Ashley Cooper was a prominent politician, social reformer and philanthropist. He was the seventh Earl of

Shaftesbury. After his death on 1 October 1885, a memorial committee was formed to erect his statue at Westminster Abbey and to fund a monument in a popular busy site in London to acknowledge Lord Shaftesbury's work for society. The committee chose Piccadilly Circus, where they built the Shaftesbury Memorial Fountain. Then, on 29 June 1893, the committee unveiled a statue of Eros perched atop the Memorial Fountain. As soon as the figure of Eros was unveiled, Piccadilly Circus became one of London's most attractive public places.

Piccadilly Circus was already a busy spot in London, connecting such famous places as Piccadilly Street, Regent Street, Shaftsbury Avenue, the Haymarket, Coventry Street and Glasshouse Street. But after the monument, with its figure of Eros, was erected, this spot became even more popular overnight. Londoners started to visit Piccadilly Circus to have a good time. Gradually, Piccadilly Circus became a place of romance; theatres, nightclubs, cinema halls, restaurants and a whole host of other entertainment venues soon flourished around it. It became a landmark of London, like Times Square in New York. Advertisements in fascinating neon lights and video displays by famous brands only add to the attraction of this hugely famous cultural spot.

There has always been some controversy about the real identity of the statue. There are people who believe that the figure on top of the Shaftesbury Memorial Fountain was meant to be the Greek god Anteros, the twin brother of Eros. Anteros was the god of selfless love, which would be appropriate to commemorate the philanthropic good deeds of the

Earl of Shaftesbury. Eros, on the other hand, was a frivolous god of romantic love' As Anteros and Eros were twins, no one could claim for sure that the figure was of either Anteros or Eros. Londoners, however, chose to accept the figure as Eros. As a result, the statue has always been popularly known as Eros.

On most Saturday evenings, I would be at Shajahan bhai's place, and I would always request Shajahan bhai and his friends to tell me anything interesting about the UK, particularly London.

One of Shajahan bhai's friends, Joti Hasan, whom we called Joti'da, was a quizmaster. He was a drama and music teacher by profession. He would often quiz everybody with tricky questions. One evening, he asked if anyone could name the first two underground stations in the world. Everybody said, 'It must be in London.' Joti'da replied, 'Well, I didn't ask for the name of a country or a city. The question was: which were the first two underground stations in the world?' Everybody kept guessing, Baker Street, Piccadilly Circus, Kings Cross, etc. After a while, Joti'da said, in smug satisfaction, 'The first two stations were Paddington and Farringdon.'

London Underground

I found many interesting stories about London Underground. After being granted permission to build an underground railway, the Metropolitan Railway company first built a test tunnel three hundred miles away from London, in a place called Kibblesworth, in Tyne and Wear, in 1855. Metropolitan worked on the test tunnel for about two years in a bid to develop the concept of an underground railway. Finally, after a series of successful test runs, on 10 January 1863, they opened the world's first underground railway in London, running between Farringdon and Paddington. The carriages of the first underground railway in the world were wooden and hauled by a steam locomotive.

The London Underground, popularly known as the Tube, gradually expanded into an extensive network and eventually added more lines until the system covered almost every corner of the city. Slowly, Londoners have become so dependent on the Underground that it would be impossible for London to function without its underground network.

British Museum

No one can exaggerate the importance of museums. Because if we turn a blind eye to history, we cannot rectify our past mistakes and progress forwards. There is a fundamental difference between reading a history book and visiting a museum. Objects are displayed in most museums to show the visitor the gradual development of the human race, covering a vast expanse of time from the prehistoric age to the present. It is vitally essential that we are familiar with our past so that we can decide on the right path toward the future.

The British Museum was not the first museum in the world by any means. However, it became the first national public museum dedicated to human history, art and culture. In those days, only the most privileged people in society had regular access to a museum. The British Museum was the first national museum in the world, giving everybody in the nation free access to it. This was made possible because the origin of the museum lies in the bequest of a famous naturalist, Sir Hans Sloane. Before he died, he made a will in which he gave all his collections, gathered over many years, to King George II, on the condition that everybody would have free access to the artefacts. And so, in 1953, Mr Sloane's private collections became the basis of the first public museum in the world. However, the modest British Museum grew in no time because, in the eighteenth century, Britain expanded its empire across the globe and became the world's dominant colonial power. As a result, over eight million objects of rare historical importance from many countries found a permanent place in the museum. The extensive collections from every continent have made it one of the wealthiest museums in the world. However, there is some controversy about how it obtained the objects in its collections. Recently, a leading British lawyer commented that the trustees of the British Museum could be considered the world's most successful receivers of stolen property.

Madame Tussauds

Before I came to London for the first time, I was looking forward to visiting Madame Tussauds at the earliest opportunity. It had been a few weeks since I first arrived in London, and yet I had not made a serious attempt to fulfil my desire to see the wonders of this wax museum. I had read so much about it. One day, at the breakfast table, my aunt enquired about which exciting places I had visited and what other places of interest I was planning to visit. I mentioned to my aunty that I had read an article about Madame Tussauds while I was in Bangladesh. I was so impressed with what I read that I promised myself that Madame Tussauds would be the first place I would see if I visited London. 'How far is Madame Tussauds?' I asked my aunt for detailed information.

My aunt smiled and said, 'It is not far at all; in fact, it is, very close to us. It has been some time since I visited Madame Tussauds. But it definitely deserves a revisit because it is so amazing, and also new characters are regularly added to the collection. So I will take you to Madame Tussauds this Sunday.'

While queuing to enter the museum, I remembered what I saw and felt when I was visiting the Louvre museum. Unlike the Louvre, Madame Tussauds did not have the luxury of occupying an enormous space. However, the place felt like a cosy environment. People coming out of the museum looked as if they had had a wonderful time. They were all smiling, laughing and patting each other, hardly talking, except repeating only one or two words,Fantastic! Amazing '.. As if words had somehow lost the power to express the extent of their satisfaction. On the other hand, people moving forward slowly in the long queue before the entrance could not hide their excitement at the prospect of experiencing something unique.

My aunt warned me that however watchful and composed I could be, the sculptures would still fool me because they all looked so real. There were statues of many well-known celebrities, and all of them seemed so natural as if they were full of life and made of blood and flesh! It was impossible to distinguish a figure made of wax from a live person. Needless to say, my experience exceeded my expectation.

Visiting Madame Tussaud's museum, I became interested to know more about Madame Tussaud herself, the person who created such a wonder to entertain others so profoundly. Many years after I visited Madame Tussauds, fortunately, a documentary film was screened on TV about the waxworks.

Born in Strasbourg, France, Madame Tussaud refused to confine herself to a closed and comfortable existence. She travelled throughout Europe, England, Scotland and Ireland, and finally settled in London to exhibit her creative talents to the world. Soon after, the young Queen Victoria allowed Madame Tussauds to make a wax model of her to display in her museum; the reputation of this wax museum spread all over the country and beyond. Gradually, Madam Tussauds became a national symbol for England. Its popularity has grown so much that the USA and many other countries, including India, have established Madame Tussaud's wax Museums of their own.

Big Ben

Big Ben has become to be the most iconic landmark of the city of London. Four identical enormous clocks, popularly known as Big Ben, occupy the top of the Elizabeth Tower at the north end of the Houses of Parliament. Big Ben is a must-see tourist attraction. The ornamented clock tower looks spectacular when the four clock faces are illuminated at night.

When I visited Big Ben, I felt that this unique structure, with its four identical, enormous clocks on each face, was not just made to tell the time. Big Ben was opened in 1859, much later than the Parliament building. I felt the primary purpose of Big Ben was to make a bold and profound statement about the British establishment. While pointing to the parliament building and the adjacent Westminster Abbey, it reminded everybody of British authority.

While I was still looking at Big Ben and the surrounding area in amazement, my concentration on the site suddenly was broken by the loud but sweet sound of the chime coming out of Big Ben. Then came the thrilling experience when Big Ben sounded three times to indicate three o'clock. I didn't know at the time that neither the Elizabeth Tower nor the four enormous clock faces were called Big Ben. That is actually the name of the heavy bell (it weighs three hundred tons) inside the clock. Nowadays, Big Ben's name indicates the enormous clock faces, the tower and the massive bell.

After appreciating the iconic Elizabeth Tower holding Big Ben, I then leisurely strolled in Parliament Square, looking at the statues of famous people, including Churchill and Gandhi.

Then I went to Westminster Bridge, at the back of the Parliament building. I walked on the bridge to reach the other side of the Thames. From there, the Parliament building and the surrounding area looked spectacular. The Parliament building appeared to have risen from the river Thames! Walking back across the bridge, I stopped in the middle to look at the river Thames. Many boats were passing by in the busy river. I noticed a few other bridges too. The bridges on the River Thames were not as ornamental and attractive as the bridges on the river Seine in Paris. However, I could imagine how stunning the view would be in the evening. I noticed a few tourist boats full of happy people having a lovely time on the river cruise. Immediately, I decided to try the river cruise boats later.

How quickly the time was passing. Big Ben chimed again and struck its massive bell four times. The sound of the bell was so loud that it could be heard from far away.

Tower Bridge

My next expedition was visiting Tower Bridge, in East London. Tower Bridge is another iconic landmark of London. It is the first bridge of its kind in the world, with a mechanism that made it possible to open up the bridge in the middle, so ships and boats with high sails could pass through. It is such a majestic structure that I couldn't be sure whether the massive crowds of tourists were attracted to this area to see the Tower of London or Tower Bridge.

The height of the bridge from the water level allowed most boats and ferries to easily pass through without the bridge opening up, disrupting the road traffic. While looking at the bridge in amazement, I realised how vast the structure was. From the riverbank, I could see two wide lanes for fast-moving cars in both directions and pavements for hundreds of pedestrians to cross the river.

I couldn't resist the temptation and walked toward the bridge. It was not surprising that the upward slope of the road towards the bridge started from a good distance away to minimise the steepness. As soon as I was on the bridge and was close to one of the twin towers, I was awestruck at the tower's massive size. These towers were highly ornamental and looked simply majestic.

The purpose of the twin towers was to hold two parallel high-level walkways at the top so that pedestrians could continue crossing the river when the bridge opened in the middle of the road. However, nowadays, because it does not take long to open and close the bridge, pedestrians do not have to wait long for the opening and closing of the bridge.

Victorian engine rooms, which open and close the middle part of the bridge, form part of the Tower Bridge Exhibition and have become tourist attractions. Visiting Tower Bridge was a very satisfying experience.

While exploring London like thirsty tourists, the High Commission office informed me that the Bangladesh Foreign Minister was in London and wanted to see us urgently. The High Commission gave me the address of the hotel where the Foreign Minister was staying and a specific time to meet him.

Unfortunately, Khokan, Babul and Akhtar had prior engagements and could not attend the meeting on such short notice. So, I went to see the Foreign Minister alone.

Upon arrival, I found the Foreign Minister talking to a group of visitors, and there was another big group waiting for him in the lobby. I informed the Foreign Minister's aide that the High Commissioner had asked me to see the Foreign Minister urgently and gave him the background to our goodwill tour. With this information, the aide let me jump the queue, allowing me to meet the Foreign Minister immediately.

His Excellency Abdus Samad Azad welcomed me and asked me to take a seat. First, he wanted to know how our tour had gone. Were there any difficult situations on the way? Were we well received by the people of the countries we visited? The chair of 'Mahila Samiti', Mrs Baksh, was in the room with a few other community leaders and party officials. She interrupted and said, 'They have done an admirable job and have made us proud. We, from the Mahila Samiti, have provided them with clothing, shoes and so on. Everybody will support them during their stay in the UK.'

I intervened and said, 'We were warmly welcomed by both the people and the government officials in all the countries we visited, starting from India and throughout Europe. We presented souvenir Bangladesh flags to the heads of state in some countries and various dignitaries, including the chief executive of the UNO, and mayors of different cities, including the mayors of Lucknow, Thessaloniki and Hamburg. Whenever the press interviewed us, we passed the goodwill message of Bangabandhu and the people of Bangladesh to the people we visited. We have received all sorts of support and cooperation from everyone everywhere.'

While talking to the Minister, I took out various documents, including our album with photographs and press cuttings. His Excellency Azad went through the papers and was very pleased with our achievements. He then found it difficult to break the bad news. 'I believe it would be great if you could continue with this tour. However, I am very sorry to have to tell you that, regrettably, the Bangladesh government can no longer sponsor the tour.' Then he said, 'You can continue with your tour without the government's sponsorship, or you can return to Bangladesh. Also, if any one of you wishes to stay here to take up a course of study, I will ask the High Commission to help you in this respect.' I was shocked to hear what he had just told me. I was so upset that I could not speak.

His Excellency Abdus Samad Azad continued, 'You do not have to make a decision immediately. Consult with your team members and inform the High Commission office of your decision in due course.'

Coming out of my meeting with the Foreign Minister, I immediately contacted Khokan, Babul and Akhtar and arranged an urgent meeting to discuss our next steps.

The news that our sponsorship would no longer continue took us aback. We had never contemplated a situation like this. While discussing what to do next, we all became disappointed and depressed that our tour was likely to end abruptly and unexpectedly.

Finally, we tried to come to terms with the situation. Although we did not know how to deal with our frustration and disappointed feelings, we all agreed that continuing the tour without government sponsorship would be extremely difficult.

We then had to consider whether to stay in the UK to study or return to Bangladesh. Khokan did not need any time to think about it. He immediately decided to return to

Bangladesh to complete his studies. However, Babul, Akhtar and I decided to take the opportunity to stay in the UK for some time to study.

The Bangladesh High Commission helped us to receive scholarships to study in the UK.

Despite our disappointment, we could still see the bright side of our goodwill mission. We all felt we had a rare opportunity to represent our country abroad, and we did it very successfully. The cycle tour from Dhaka to London was quite challenging. However, we were on a noble mission to represent our country abroad, which was very inspiring. It gave us tremendous courage and the strength to complete the tour successfully.

We were overwhelmed when we heard the story of schoolchildren who had worked hard to raise funds and collected various objects for the Bangladeshi refugees during the liberation war. We felt proud when we met people in different countries who shared our happiness that we were independent and our trouble was over.

We were, and still are, proud to have had such a wonderful opportunity to represent our country abroad and, at the same time, to gain the most valuable experience of our lifetimes. Joy Bangla!

The End

About the author

Jamal Hasan Lives in London. He left Bangladesh with three friends on a world cycle tour as a goodwill mission to thank the people of the world for supporting the liberation war of 1971. The Bangladesh Foreign Ministry, Dhaka University, and the Bangladesh Sports Federation sponsored this goodwill mission.

During the late 1970s, Jamal Hasan became a leading anti-racist activist in East London. He served as the General Secretary of the Action Committee Against Racial Attacks, which organised a National Demonstration, after the racist murder of a Bengali factory worker, Altab Ali, on 4 May 1978.

Jamal Hasan is retired, having worked all his life as an Immigration law practitioner at Law Centres in London. As a result, Jamal Hasan had the direct experience of listening to hundreds of his clients about their pain and agony of being separated from their loved ones by the harsh British immigration rules. These heartbreaking stories inspired him to write a novel, 'The Disclosure', in 2020.

The Author's First Book

The Disclosure

'The Disclosure' is a fiction where the author skilfully describes events which seem so remote from daily life, but yet, the readers feel they are given a realistic visual description of the main character, Jahir Sarkar's, journey through the unpredictable path of his life.

The story starts with a mysterious opening, and the theme of curiosity is maintained throughout until the very end. The readers are absorbed with a light-hearted and entertaining narrative of a series of events in the life of Jahir Sarkar as he chases his dream and achieves success.

The Disclosure contains a number of plots and sub-plots. It describes the social issues surrounding conflicts between different religious and ethnic communities. The Disclosure gives a strong and convincing message that conflicts between communities are often engineered by politicians for their political agenda and that people from diverse backgrounds can live together in harmony. One of the interesting aspects of the Disclosure is that it describes a fascinating rural culture of Bangladesh which is on the verge of being forgotten as modernisation takes place.

Ansar Ahmed Ullah
Bisshobanglanews24.com

Printed in Great Britain
by Amazon

18202121R10171